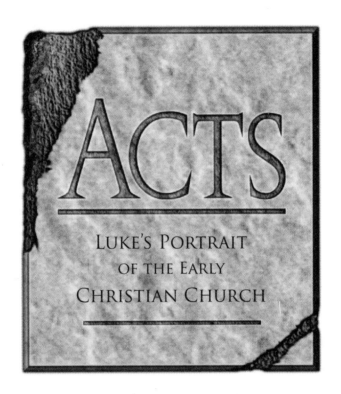

ACTS

LUKE'S PORTRAIT
OF THE EARLY
CHRISTIAN CHURCH

BENNIE GOODWIN, PH.D. AND
CHAPLAIN MELODY GOODWIN, D.MIN.

Urban Ministries, Inc.
CHICAGO, ILLINOIS

Acts:
Luke's Portrait of the Early Christian Church

Scripture quotations are from *Today's English Version of the Bible* unless otherwise stated.

GOOD NEWS TRANSLATION, SECOND EDITION, Copyright© 1992 by American Bible Society. Used by permission. All rights reserved.

Published by UMI (Urban Ministries, Inc.)
ISBN: 0-932715-54-1
Library of Congress Control Number: 2005904659
Printed in the United States of America.

CONTENTS

*This book is dedicated to my daughters,
Mary Ellen and Constance Marie.*

INTRODUCTION

The book of Acts is a very exciting and unique piece of New Testament literature. The New Testament begins with four Gospel accounts that are somewhat alike, and closes with letters by various persons that, while different, are also similar. But there is no book in the New Testament like the book of Acts. As the history book of the New Testament, it is in a class by itself.

Jesus Christ is the central figure of all the New Testament, including the book of Acts. The Gospel accounts tell of His life and teachings. The letters focus on the issues, problems, and concerns of those who were called by His name; and Acts links the Gospel accounts and letters together by recounting the expansion of the early Christian Church. Each of these types of literature is important, and the New Testament can be understood and interpreted accurately only when we grasp the relationship between its three sections.

Style

This book is written with laypersons in mind—especially teachers of Sunday School, Bible School, Vacation Bible School, and other nonprofessional Christian Education workers. We hope this book will be a help as you prepare leaders for future service.

This is not a technically written book. To read this book, you do not need *Webster's Dictionary* in one hand, a Bible dictionary in the other, and commentaries and Bible atlases scattered on your desk or around your feet. It is written simply, clearly, and interestingly. It is meant to bless you, not to test your endurance. Read it with excitement in your heart and a prayer on your lips.

Structure

Like the New Testament, this book, *Acts: Luke's Portrait of the Early Christian Church*, is also divided into three parts. Part I consists of two short chapters, one on the book of Acts and the other about Luke, whom we believe to be its author.[1] Part II is a longer section and focuses on the persons and ministries of Peter, Paul, and some other prominent persons in Acts. The final and most extensive part discusses Luke's Portrait of the Early Church as a Christ-directed, Spirit-empowered worshiping, ministering, and expanding movement. The book closes with a look at the first century Christian Church as a model for the Black Church of the 21st century. We think you're going to be encouraged and challenged by the thoughts that this book will inspire.

How to Use This Book

1. This book may be used as a teaching tool or study guide to help you enrich the mental and spiritual lives of your students—particularly where the lessons are focused in the book of Acts.

2. You may also use this book as a Sunday School or VBS elective course. That is, instead of using your regular adult or young adult curriculum, this book may be used as a substitute text; or you may ask each student or each family to purchase a copy of this book and use it as a class supplement, research tool, or suggested book for additional weekly reading.

3. In addition, this book may be used as part of your personal or family devotions, as a lunchtime Bible study guide at work, or as a "book club" selection for a teacher's fellowship at school.

These are a few of the many ways that *Acts: Luke's Portrait of the Early Christian Church* might be used to enhance your knowledge and spiritual growth. You will probably think of other uses as you read and study its content.

Today's English Version (TEV)

Today's English Version (TEV) is the version that is quoted most often in this book. The TEV is probably the simplest, clearest, most nontechnical version available. It expresses the stories, incidents, and episodes in the language that many of us use when we preach, teach, or write. We revere the old King James Version. It's the version we were brought up on, the version from which our parents, Sunday School teachers and Vacation Bible School leaders taught us to memorize the Scriptures. But we don't speak as King James and his translators did in the 1600s. If you like, read this book and the TEV along with your King James Version and let the total experience build your faith and love for the Lord Jesus Christ.

How to Get the Most Out of This Book

1. First look at the contents page. Select a chapter that sounds especially interesting to you. Turn to it and read it—just for pleasure.

2. Repeat the process until you've read all of the "special interest" chapters. Then find a *Today's English Version* (TEV) of the Bible, also called the *Good News for Modern Man.* Turn to Acts; flip through the chapters; and read the stories, incidents, and episodes that catch your attention.

3. Come back to this book, begin with Chapter 1 and read it all the way through in one sitting, if possible.

4. Go back to the TEV and do the same with the book of Acts. At this point, you will begin to see Luke as a Spirit-inspired man who intelligently organized this history of the early church. You might also see how it fits between the Gospel accounts and the New Testament letters. You will perceive early Christians as real people who lived real lives, confronted real problems, and experienced real defeats and victories. Luke is a wonderful writer. We would not be surprised if Acts became one of your favorite books. As you read it more often and make its principles a part of your daily life, you'll appreciate it more and share it with your family, friends, and others to whom you minister.

PART I
Acts: Book And Author

Both the Old and New Testaments consist of three basic sections. The Old Testament may be divided into history (Genesis through Esther), poetry (Job through Song of Solomon), and prophecy (Isaiah through Malachi). The New Testament begins with the Gospel accounts (Matthew through John) and concludes with the letters (Romans through Revelation), with the one book of history (Acts) connecting the two sections. In this section of *Acts: Luke's Portrait of the Early Christian Church*, we will briefly give some background about the book of Acts, and Luke, its author.

1
Acts, Book Of History

1. The Title

Over the almost 2,000 years of its existence, the book of Acts has been given many titles. It seems that Luke did not give it a title, and so various persons have given it titles of their own. Many scholars believe it was first referred to by the single word *Acts*, which in Greek means "deeds"—good or bad. Later it was called, The Acts, Acts of the Apostles, Acts of the Holy Apostles, and Acts of the Apostolic Men. A man named Oecumenius called it The Gospel of the Holy Spirit. In the King James (KJV) and *Revised Standard* (RSV) versions, it is called The Acts of the Apostles, while in the *New International Version* (NIV) and the *Living Bible* (LB), it is simply called Acts.[2]

Some writers have noted that although all of the apostles are mentioned at least once (Acts 1:12–13), all of them except Peter, James, and John are only mentioned once. Acts is primarily about what Jesus Christ, as the Holy Spirit, did through the "two prominent Ps"—Peter (Acts 1–12) and Paul (Acts 13–28).

Keeping the facts in mind that Luke apparently didn't name his book, and that it is primarily about Jesus Christ, the Holy Spirit, Peter, and Paul, you are at liberty to choose among the titles or to compose one that you think best fits the book's contents. We have chosen "A History of the Early Christian Church" for our official title, but for the sake of variety, we will use other titles as well.

2. Date and Place

As in the case of Luke's Gospel account, we do not know when or where Luke's "History of the Early Christian Church" was written. Various dates as early as A.D. 60 and as late as the first part of the second century (A.D. 100–110) have been suggested.

It was certainly written after Luke's Gospel account (Acts 1:1), which we believe to have been written around A.D. 63. But it does not mention Paul's martyrdom, believed to have taken place around between A.D. 67 or 68; nor does it mention the destruction of Jerusalem, which is known to have taken place in A.D. 70. Therefore, we believe a date after A.D. 63 and before A.D. 70 to be a somewhat safe, through uncertain, date. I. Howard Marshall in his book *The Acts of the Apostles* suggests that "a date toward . . . shortly before or after 70 A.D." to be a defensible date.[3]

The place where Luke wrote his "History" is even more uncertain. Such places as Antioch, Ephesus, and Rome have been suggested. Because Luke closes his book with events that took place in Rome, it is a popular "place of writing" among speculators.

3. Purpose

Why was Acts written? Luke implies at least a part of the answer in his brief introduction (1:1–11).

1. He wanted to finish the former "treatise" (KJV), "letter" (LB), or "book" (NIV, RSV) he had written to Theophilus (1:1). He had started a story that did not end with his Gospel account. He recognized that Jesus had not finished His work. In the Gospel accounts, Jesus had "[begun] . . . to do and teach" (KJV); in Acts, the Lord continued this work, so Luke wanted to tell the rest of the story.

2. Luke wanted to tell how the disciples fulfilled Jesus' command (Acts 1:8). He wanted to tell the dramatic story of how the Gospel was carried from Jerusalem, the tiny capital of Judaism, to the international capital of the Roman Empire. He wanted to show how a spiritual virus began with 120 people in a second-story room and spread like an epidemic until thousands throughout the Empire were infected.

3. Luke wanted to illustrate that the Gospel has universal appeal. Many in Israel, even Peter, whom Jesus gave "keys of the Kingdom" (Matthew 16:19) thought that Jesus' message was just for the Jews. Luke dramatized in his "History" that the Gospel was for the

world—for poor and rich; men and women; soldiers and civilians; government officials and ordinary citizens; Jews and Gentiles; and Asians, Africans, and Europeans.

4. Luke wrote to inform. It is believed that some of Paul's letters had been or were being written and that perhaps at least three of the Gospel accounts (Matthew, Mark, and Luke) had already been written. Acts forms a bridge between the Gospel accounts and the New Testament letters. Acts tells a story that gives the Gospel accounts continuity, and the letters greater clarity and coherence.[4]

5. Luke's "History" not only tells of the outward growth of the church, but also its inward development. It recounts how questions and conflicts arose and were settled. It tells how deacons were appointed, Christian education was implemented, communion was observed, and missionaries were commissioned and sent out. We would certainly like to know more, but we appreciate Luke for telling us as much as he does about how the church started, grew, and developed.

6. Luke relates the Christian church to the Roman government. Luke's "History" has often been called an "apology" or defense. Luke presents Christianity as a legitimate form of Judaism and its proper fulfillment. In the Roman Empire, most religions including Judaism were tolerated. Luke presents Christianity as an outgrowth of Judaism, and therefore deserving of the Roman government's toleration and protection. In fact, Luke notes several instances where Christianity was well received and approved by Roman officials. As we shall see, the opposition to the presentation of the Gospel message usually came from Jews, not Romans or other Gentiles.

7. A final purpose of Luke's "History" is the presentation of a pattern or model. Did Luke foresee the need for a rapidly growing church to have a written document by which to guide itself and teach its children and new converts? Did he foresee the time when Christians would be asking:

> Should people of different ethnic groups and
> nationalities be members of the same local church?

> What should be the relationship between
> Christian men and women in ministry?
> Should women be preachers?
>
> Should Christians be sent out to present the
> Gospel in non-Christian cities and regions?
>
> How should the Church settle its internal
> disputes?

While Luke has not given us a Book of Order, or a detailed church manual, he has given us a very helpful reference book in story form that has proven useful as a teaching instrument for almost 20 centuries. Thank the Lord for all who participated in the Christian church's teaching-learning process, and especially for Dr. Luke who preserved a record of early church history and Christian education. In his record, we find information, instructions, and inspiration.

4. Structure

Luke focuses his "History" on two prominent human beings—Peter and Paul. His book "falls into" two "natural" divisions. Part I focuses on Peter (chapters 1–12), and Part II focuses on Paul (chapters 13–28). However, there are other ways of organizing Luke's story for study and analysis. This outline by Dr. Ralph Earle is appealing. It is brief and focuses on the "witnessing" theme:[5]

> I. Witnessing in Jerusalem 1–7
> II. Witnessing in Judea and Samaria 8–12
> III. Witnessing in the Gentile World 13–28

If we fill in these three main headings, an outline like the following would emerge:

> I. Witnessing in Jerusalem 1–7
> A. Introduction (1:1–26)
> B. Pentecost and the Healing of the Lame
>   Man (2:1–3:26)

C. The First Persecution (4:1–37)

D. Ananias and Sapphira (5:1–42)

E. The First Deacons (6:1–7:60)

II. Witnessing in Judea and Samaria 8–12

A. Philip, the Evangelist (8:1–25)

B. Saul's Conversion (9:1–31)

C. Peter and the Gentiles (10:1–11:18)

D. Christians at Antioch (11:19–30)

E. Peter's Deliverance and Herod's Death (12:1–25)

III. Witnessing in the Gentile World 13–28

A. Paul and Barnabas: Their First Missionary Journey (13:1–14:28)

B. The Jerusalem Council (15:1–35)

C. Paul's Second and Third Missionary Journeys (15:36–21:16)

D. Paul at Jerusalem and Caesarea (21:17–26:32)

E. Paul's Voyage and Stay in Rome (27:1–28:31)

5. Summary of Contents

I. Introduction (Chapter 1)

Under the inspiration of the Holy Spirit, Luke thoughtfully and systematically sets the stage for his "History of the Early Christian Church." After addressing it to Theophilus to give it an unmistakable connection to his Gospel account, he seems to raise and answer at least five important questions about the Church.

1. Who will be the central Person of the Church? The answer is Jesus Christ, the Person who lived, died, rose again, ascended, and will come again for the Church (vv. 1–3, 9–11). He is the Person who leads the Church and provides its purpose, plan, and power.

2. What is the Church's purpose and plan? Jesus told His disciples to be His witnesses. That was their purpose in life, and the plan they were to follow was to begin in Jerusalem and to move outward to the farthest part of the earth (v. 8).

3. What is the Church's source of power? Since the Church's task is spiritual, the source of its power is also spiritual—not eco-

nomic, political, social, or military, but spiritual. The Church, while recognizing alternative power sources, is to rely on spiritual power to do its spiritual work.

4. How is the Church to receive guidance? When Jesus was present in body, the disciples went to Jesus and He gave them guidance (see 1:6–8). After He ascended, they looked to the Scriptures (1:16–20), talked with Him through prayer (1:14, 24–25), and remembered and imitated His words and actions (1:21–22; 3:6–7).

5. Who should be involved in implementing the Church's program of evangelism and missions? People—men and women, apostles and laity, individuals and families, the well-known and "unknown" (1:13–14). There is a place for all believers in the work of the kingdom of God (v. 3). Should someone become disabled, fall, or defect for some reason (1:15–26), others are chosen to take their places and carry on the work of the Lord until the Good News has reached the farthest part of the earth.

Luke sets the stage for one of the most exciting stories in all literature—the carrying of the Gospel from the tiny little city of Jerusalem to Rome, the center of world power.

II. Witnessing in Jerusalem (Chapters 2–7)

The Church's witness started with a literal BANG! The disciples followed Jesus' instructions and waited in the Upper Room for His power. Suddenly they were aware of His presence as they had never been before. It exploded on them like thunder and lightning, and spilled all out into the streets of the neighborhood. Old cussing, fussing, fighting Peter was transformed into an eloquent preacher and 3,000 people were swept into the Church.

In chapter 3, the excitement continued as a lame man was healed and went jumping and shouting into the temple. This exciting episode was followed by the Church's first recorded series of problems. In chapters 4–7, the Church experienced its first persecution, display of God's anger, internal strife, and martyrdom.

III. Witnessing in Judea and Samaria (Chapters 8–12)

As a result of persecution, the Church was pushed into its second stage of growth. As Christians fled from Jerusalem, they "scattered" throughout the regions of Judea and Samaria and "went everywhere, preaching the message" (8:1, 4). As a result of the preaching of Philip, the Samaritans and a high African official heard the Gospel (8:1–40). In the meantime, Stephen was stoned and Saul was converted (7:54–60; 9:1–31). Peter began preaching to Gentiles and the people in Antioch gave "us" the title "Christians" (9:32–11:26), by which we are still identified.

IV. Witnessing in the Gentile World (Chapters 13–28)

This section of Luke's "History" focuses on what the Holy Spirit did through the apostle Paul. After he was commissioned by the Antioch Church, he went on three important evangelistic tours, interrupted by two important council meetings in Jerusalem (15:1–35; 21:17–23:35). Luke closes this final section by recounting their voyage to Rome and ends his story there. Tradition says that it was in Rome that Paul was killed by the orders of Nero, the mentally ill Roman emperor. Using his interesting and exciting storytelling method, Luke told how the disciples carried out Jesus' commission to be His witnesses in Jerusalem, Judea, Samaria, and to the uttermost parts of the world.

2
Luke, The Writer

Isn't it amazing the facts we don't know about things that are important to us? That's the condition we find ourselves in when we ask who was the author of the book of Acts. When was he born and where? We really don't know. We don't have a record of his birth or the testimony of a person, who could say, "I was there," or knew someone who was there.

The closest persons to Luke, who left information for us, are the early church fathers who were the links between Jesus, His disciples, and those who lived in the second and third centuries.[6]

1. Date and Place of Birth

An early church source, the *Anti-Marcionite Prologue*, states that Luke was born in Antioch and died, unmarried and childless, in Bocotia at the age of 84.[7] St. Jerome, an early church father, called Luke a Syrian, born in Antioch.[8] Again we have to confess that we really don't know precisely when or where Luke was born.

Paul is the first and only New Testament writer to mention Luke. We know from Philemon 23–24 that Luke worked with Paul, who called him one of his "fellow workers." And we know that when Paul sent his other assistants to various cities, he would have been all alone, except that Luke was with him (2 Timothy 4:9–11).

2. Paul's Traveling Companion

Other evidence of a connection between Paul and Luke are the so-called "we" passages in the book of Acts. In at least three places in Acts, the writer slips into first person plural. Instead of saying "they," he says "we" (Acts 16:10–17; 20:5–21:18; 27:1–28:16). If, as we believe, the author of both Luke and Acts is Luke, then Luke was with Paul in Philippi (Acts 16:10–17), Troas (20:5–12), Mitylene (20:14), Samos and Miletus (20:15), Cos, Rhodes, and Patara (21:1),

Tyre (21:3), Ptolemais (21:7), Caesarea (21:8–16), and Jerusalem (21:17–18).

The final "we" passage puts Paul, Aristarchus, and Luke together on their way to Rome (27:1–2). They arrived there after sailing by way of Sidon (27:3), Myra (27:5), Crete (27:7), Malta (also called Melita, 28:1), Syracuse (28:12), and Puteoli, an Italian port (28:13).[9]

3. A Medical Doctor

Paul's letter to the Colossians reveals that Luke was a doctor, "the beloved physician" (Colossians 4:14, KJV). *The Muratorian Canon*, an early church document, also called Luke a physician who wrote the gospel of Luke and the book of Acts.[10] Earlier Bible scholars thought they detected special medical language in Luke's writing. After more research, it was suggested that Luke's language was not special but "that the language used in Luke and Acts to describe ailments and cures is compatible with the ancient tradition that the author was a doctor."[11]

4. A Gentile

It is believed by some writers that Luke was also a Gentile and therefore the only non-Jewish writer of a New Testament book. This belief is based on Colossians 4:10 and 4:14. There Paul first sends greetings from his Jewish assistants, calling them "of the circumcision" (4:11, KJV). Then he speaks of Luke and Demas (4:14), whom it may be assumed are Gentiles and not "of the circumcision." Other scholars point to Luke's special interest in Gentiles in both Luke and Acts and his fluency in the Greek language.[12] Commentator Albert Barnes confirmed that although Luke was "intimately acquainted with Jewish rites, customs, opinions, and prejudices," he was a Jewish-Christian convert "born of Gentile parents."[13]

5. Compassionate

One of the qualities that comes through in Luke's writings is his social consciousness and his "inexhaustible sympathy for the troubles of other people."[14] His story of Jesus is sometimes called the "Gospel of the underdog."[15] Whether the victim is a woman, a child, a tax collector, or a Samaritan, Luke is interested and sympathetic. He presents Jesus and the apostles as concerned servants of the sick, the helpless, and hopeless. He has an eye for the hurting and a heart for their needs.

6. Historian

I. Howard Marshall has said in *Luke: Historian & Theologian*, "The task of the historian is to reconstruct the past, to give an account of events as they actually happened."[16] That is what Luke sets out to do. Luke was not an eyewitness disciple, so he had to do what many historians are required to do. He had to conduct research. He said in his introduction, "I have carefully studied all these matters from their beginning" in order to "write an orderly account . . ." (Luke 1:3). He did such an outstanding job that his Gospel account has been called "the best life of Christ ever written," and a "product of the most careful historical research."[17] He probably interviewed many people, including Jesus' mother, and if the "we" passages were written by Luke, he surely knew Peter and James (Acts 15:13–14). It's not hard to imagine Dr. Luke going around the Jerusalem Council meetings with scroll in hand, asking questions, and gathering and confirming information for his book.

7. Theologian

Luke was not only interested in the facts; he was also interested in the meaning of the facts. He promised Theophilus an "orderly account" but also the "full truth" (Luke 1:4). That meant Luke had to interpret the facts. He had to select the facts and events and put them together so that Jesus' ministry in his Gospel account and Acts could be clearly perceived and received. He was not only interested in what happened, but in why it happened and what the results were. Luke not only records that Jesus ascended into heaven, but that the disciples worshiped Him and went back into Jerusalem filled with great joy. There they spent their time in the temple, giving thanks to God (Luke 24:50–53). Through Luke's selection of facts and events, he disclosed their meaning.

8. Storyteller

Luke's basic writing style was storytelling. Seldom is Luke's voice heard. He recounts his history and does his interpretation through the voices of others. Nowhere does he call Jesus' birth the "Virgin Birth." He simply tells of the conversation between an angel and a virgin and records the outcome (Luke 1:26–38). Nowhere does he discuss the doctrine of divine "faith" healing. He simply tells story after story of miraculous healing (Acts 3:1–9; 9:33–42; 13:6–12). Nowhere does he discuss demonology. He just shows Jesus healing "Mr. Legion" (Luke 8:26–39) and casting out demons through His followers (Acts 5:16). Nowhere does Luke expound the doctrine of forgiveness—even last-minute, deathbed salvation. But he does record Jesus forgiving a sinner while on the Cross and promising to take a dying thief into "paradise" (Luke 23:39–43).

Even though we don't know when or where Luke was born, we thank God for anointing this compassionate Gentile physician, who gave the Church and the world accurate history and superb Christian theology in stories.

PART II
Luke's Portrait Of Church Leaders

In this section we want to look at Luke's portrait of church leaders in three dimensions. First we want to focus on Luke's biographical and character sketches of Peter and Paul; next we want to look at their major ministries. Finally we want to give brief sketches of some of the other persons who were leaders in the early Christian Church.

3
Portrait Of Peter:
A Biographical Sketch

There are several biographical sketches in the Old Testament. Moses' self-portrait is perhaps the most complete, followed by his portraits of Abraham, Jacob, and Joseph. Samuel gives us his autobiographical sketch and a portrait of David's early life. Someone has left us a brief "life of Solomon."

In the New Testament, there are no biographies in any complete sense of the word. Matthew, Mark, and Luke's portraits of Jesus are exceptions, although we surely wish we had much more information about Him, especially about those 18 years between His temple visit and the beginning of His ministry. We have no such portrait of Peter, but let's piece together the information we have.

1. Peter in the Gospels

Peter was called by more than one name. The name given to him by his family was Simon or Simeon (Acts 15:14; 2 Peter 1:1). When he met Jesus, Jesus changed his name to Peter (Mark 3:16; Luke 6:14). In Aramaic, the language most commonly spoken in Palestine, the name Cephas or Peter means "rock." So from then on, Jesus and the disciples perhaps nicknamed Simon Peter, "Rocky."

It seems that "Rocky" was probably born in Bethsaida (John 1:44), as were James and John, but later moved with his father, Jonah or John, and his brother Andrew to Capernaum. Sometime before meeting Jesus, he married (Mark 1:30; 1 Corinthians 9:5) and became a part of his father's fishing business (Mark 1:16; Luke 5:1–11). Peter's father and Zebedee, the father of James and John, must have been business partners or at least close friends (Matthew 4:18–22; Mark 1:16–20; Luke 5:1–11).

Peter had at least one brother, Andrew, who introduced him to Jesus. Both of them became early followers of John the Baptist, but it was Andrew who announced to Peter, "We have found the Messiah" (John 1:40–42). Their ministry with Jesus began a lifetime of challenges and commitments that dramatically changed the direction of their lives. Luke tells us that after an all-night, futile fishing episode, Jesus called Peter and his brother to become fishers of men (Luke 5:1–11). From that time forward, Peter seems to have become Jesus' assistant leader. He was part of the three-man inner circle, led all four of the lists of disciples (Matthew 10:2–4; Mark 3:16–19; Luke 6:13–16; Acts 1:13), and usually spoke for the other disciples when important questions were raised. Sometimes he spoke without having complete or accurate information, and one time he even rebuked Jesus (Matthew 16:22). At another time he denied he knew Jesus, but what Peter said and did often reflected the thoughts and feelings of the other 11 disciples. Peter repented for having denied Jesus (Luke 22:62), and though all of the Gospel writers recorded the denial (Matthew 26:57–58; Mark 14:53–54; Luke 22:57; John 18:17, 25–27), Jesus treated it as if it had never happened and never referred to it as having occurred.

2. Peter in Acts

In Luke's "History," Peter is still the leader. He was the person who called the disciples together to elect a person to take Judas's place (Acts 1:15–26). Peter preached the first sermon on Pentecost Sunday, when 3,000 people joined the Church (2:14–41). The Lord used him and John to heal a lame man (3:1–10), and he was God's instrument of healing to many others in Jerusalem (5:12–16), Lydda, and Joppa (9:32–41).

Peter's preaching caused him and the other disciples to face the Jewish Council (4:1–22). Later they were arrested again, and whipped but miraculously delivered from prison (5:17–19). This was the same Peter who pronounced judgment on a couple who tried to impress the Church by deceit (5:3–11), and the same Peter who almost "cussed out" Simon, the magician, for trying to buy

Holy Spirit power (8:20). This was the same Peter who used "the keys" that Jesus had given him (Matthew 16:19) to admit some Caesarean Gentiles to the kingdom (Acts 10:34–48). He watched them receive the Holy Spirit and defended their right to be accepted as Christians at the Jerusalem Council (15:7–11).

After the council meeting, Peter dropped out of sight but he must have continued to minister, especially in Corinth where there was a "Peter Party" (Galatians 2:11–14) and in Rome where Tertullian, a second century African church leader, mentioned that Peter died for his faith in Christ under the rule of Emperor Nero.[18]

During these "unrecorded years," Peter probably visited believers in Pontus, Galatia, Cappadocia, Asia, and Bithynia (1 Peter 1:1). These were provinces in Asia Minor between the Taurus Mountains and the Black Sea to whom Peter wrote two letters (1 and 2 Peter) that have been preserved in the New Testament. He probably wrote these letters while in the city of Rome.

4
Portrait Of Peter:
A Character Sketch

We have traced Peter's life from his birthplace in Bethsaida, to Capernaum, to Jerusalem, and finally to Rome where we believe he wrote his letters and died for his faith. The Lord used Peter to lead, preach, heal, defend his faith, and write letters of encouragement. But what kind of person was Peter in terms of character? What were his outstanding qualities?

1. In the Gospels

In spite of the fact that Jesus called him "Rocky," Luke showed Peter to be a combination of sand and rock. On the one hand, he was concerned about his mother-in-law (Luke 4:38–39), but on the other hand, he was ready to cut off a servant's head! He wasn't really after the man's ear. A quick shift in head position saved the man's life (Luke 22:50). Although Luke was kind and did not name Peter as the culprit, we know who cut off the ear of the High Priest's servant from John's account of the episode (John 18:10).

Peter was *responsive but impulsive.* He sometimes spoke because he felt something needed to be said, but without thinking things through. On the Mount of Transfiguration (Luke 9:28–36), the scene was so awe-inspiring that Peter sensed some expression was needed. But Luke records that Peter spoke without "really (knowing) what he was saying" (v. 33). Peter responded to the situation, but in an impulsive manner. The voice from heaven told him to be quiet and listen to Jesus (v. 35).

Peter was *trusting but fearful.* When Jesus asked Peter to let Him use his boat so that He could better teach the crowd, Peter immediately trusted Jesus with his boat (Luke 5:3–11). When Jesus called Peter to leave his occupation to follow Him, he immediately "left all" to follow Jesus (Luke 5:10; 18:28, NIV). Luke shows that Peter trusted Jesus with his possessions and time. But when someone identified him as one of Jesus' disciples while Jesus was on trial, he denied knowing who Jesus was (Luke 22:54–62). Peter trusted Jesus but it seemed that when Jesus chose not to defend Himself, Peter was scared and "petered out."

Peter was *assertive and repentant.* When he saw Jesus walking on the water, he was so assertive that he asked Jesus to let him walk on the water too. But when he started to sink, he was repentant enough to say, "Lord, save me!" (Matthew 14:30, NIV). He was so assertive that he told Jesus He was wrong for predicting that Peter would deny Him (Matthew 26:35). Peter declared that he was ready to go to prison and even to die with Jesus (Luke 22:33). But when he did deny Jesus, he went out and repented with bitter tears (22:62).

With all of Peter's ups and downs, it seems that his most "rock-like" quality was his *availability.* He was always there. When Jesus needed a boat or a follower, Peter was there. When Jesus was on the stormy sea, Transfiguration mountain, or in the courtroom, Peter was there. Only at the Cross is there no record of Peter's presence, but on Resurrection morning, Luke records that the first disciple to enter the tomb was Peter (24:12). His character had not yet attained its true "rock-like" hardness, but the potential was there.

> He was "sometimes up, and sometimes down,
> and sometimes almost level with the ground."
>
> But he was usually present, active, and
> accounted for.

2. In Acts

In the Gospel accounts, we see a very human Peter, a Peter struggling to be better, struggling to live up to the new name that Jesus gave him. We see him rising and falling, walking and crawling, learning, growing and maturing. In Acts we meet the same man. but he's different. Peter has been with Jesus for three or more years. Peter has experienced His holy power. He is still responsive and somewhat impulsive, as seen in his apparent impulsive response to physical (Acts 3:1–8; 9:32–41) and spiritual needs (1:15–26; 2:14ff.; 10:47–48), but his responses and impulses are now under the *control of the Spirit.*

Peter is still trusting, but is no longer fearful. *He is bold.* Luke reports that when he stood before the Jewish Council, they "were amazed to see how bold Peter and John were" (v. 13). And when they were told not "to speak to anyone in the name of Jesus" (v. 17), Peter and John answered, "We cannot stop speaking of what we ourselves have seen and heard" (v. 20). Later Peter boldly pronounced judgment on Ananias and Sapphira (5:1–11) and warned Simon the magician to change his thinking (8:20–24).

In Acts, Peter is still *available* to serve the Lord—whether in Jerusalem, Samaria, Lydda, Joppa, Sharon (9:32–43), or Caesarea (10:1–48). But there is an added quality to his availability. Luke captures it when he notes that after the Council "called the apostles in, had them whipped, and ordered them never again to speak in the name of Jesus," they set the apostles free (5:40). And then Luke adds this phrase, "As the apostles left the Council, they were happy" (v. 41). *Happy?* Yes, happy—"because God had considered them worthy to suffer disgrace for the sake of Jesus" (v. 41). This is a new Peter. Not only is he responsive, trusting, available, and bold but now he's full of joy—even when his back is bloody.

> Faith of our Fathers living still,
> In spite of dungeon fire and sword:
> O how our hearts beat high with joy
> Whene'er we hear that glorious word!
> Faith of our fathers, holy faith!
> We will be true to Thee 'til death![19]

Peter is one of our favorite Bible characters because we are so much like him. In the Gospel accounts, he often expresses what we really feel and makes us laugh and cry at the "Peter" in us. But he gives us hope. We know that if Peter can change, so can we. And when we see the mature Christian he became in the book of Acts, we know that through the control of the Spirit, we too can rise to new spiritual heights!

5
Portrait Of Paul:
A Biographical Sketch

The other main character in Acts is Paul. Our four primary sources of information about Paul are: (1) Luke's book of Acts, (2) Paul's New Testament letters, (3) a few statements in other New Testament literature, and (4) traditions found in written sources outside of the Bible.

We are endeavoring to see Luke's portrait of Paul. Therefore we will mention other sources, but our focus will be on what Luke tells us about Paul in the book of Acts. We will ask and attempt to answer the same questions we used in our biographical and character sketches of Peter—who was he (biography), and what was he really like (character)?

1. Name
Before his conversion on the Damascus Road (Acts 9:1–8), Paul was known as Saul. In fact, it was not until he began his first evangelistic tour in Acts 13 that Luke began to use Paul, the name by which he is most widely known today. His Hebrew or Jewish name was *Sha'ul* or Saul; *Paulus* or Paul was his Latin or Roman name. Saul means "asked for" and Paul means "little."

2. Birth
We do not know the year of his birth. Some say he was born around A.D. 3, while John H. Hayes writes that he was born around the "beginning of the (first) century" or about the same time as Jesus' birth.[20] We do know from Paul's own statement that he was born in Tarsus, a Greek city and the capital of Cilicia in the area of Asia Minor (Acts 21:39).

Tarsus was located at the mouth of the Cydnus River and through the city ran a major East-West trade route, making it a thriving commercial, educational, and cultural center. Paul described it as "no mean city" (v. 39, KJV, RSV). That was his way of saying that Tarsus was not a little "one stop sign, hick town."

3. Family

According to Jerome, a prominent church father writing in the fourth century A.D., Paul's parents were originally from Gischala, a Jewish town in Galilee. At some point before Paul's birth, they moved to Tarsus and earned or bought their Roman citizenship. Therefore Paul was born a Roman citizen. He was both a "Hebrew of Hebrews," that is, a Jew born of Jewish parents, not a convert to Judaism, and a Roman citizen, born of Roman parents. This was a dual heritage of which he seemed very proud. We do not know his parents' names or how many brothers and sisters he might have had. We know he had at least one sister and one nephew, whom he refers to as living in Jerusalem at the time of one of his arrests (23:16).

4. Education

Paul's education had several dimensions. The first dimension was his home training. He doesn't tell us, but we know that all Jewish parents were commanded to teach their sons the Old Testament Scriptures, the laws of God, and a trade. Paul tells us that his father was a Pharisee (23:6). Certainly he carried out a Jewish father's responsibilities—to circumcise each son, to teach him the Law by having him memorize Scripture and Jewish history, and to teach him a trade (Deuteronomy 6:4–9, 20–25).

Why tent making (Acts 18:3)? We don't know precisely, but we do know that Tarsus was a center for the manufacturing of a coarse goat's hair material used to make tents. The abundant availability of this material and jobs in tent making might have influenced his father's decision. The goat's hair material was not only used to make tents, but awnings for businesses and sails for boats.[21]

The second dimension of Paul's education took place in the *synagogue*. There the Jewish boy's home training was confirmed and extended. In the synagogue, they learned Jewish law, history, and rituals in greater depth as they prepared to be bar mitzvahed or to become sons of the Law at the age of 13.

Study with Rabbi Gamaliel, the grandson of the highly esteemed

Rabbi Hillel, was the third dimension of Paul's education. It was probably during his time in Jerusalem with Gamaliel that Paul developed his knowledge of Greek language and literature, philosophy, and religion. Luke gives us a brief glimpse of Paul's teacher in Acts 5:34–39. Undoubtedly Paul received superior instruction with this Jewish scholar, who was recognized as "the most famous rabbinic teacher of the day." Gamaliel's handling of the angry Sanhedrin, who were ready to kill the apostles, demonstrates why he was said to be "liberal in mind and tolerant in spirit."

A fourth dimension of Paul's education came after his conversion, and is sometimes called his "Arabian experience." We can only speculate about what Paul did when he "went into Arabia" (Galatians 1:17, KJV), but it is said that he probably "spent much time in the study and re-study of Scripture, and in prayer" preparing for his Gentile ministry to which the Lord had called him during his conversion experience. His years in Arabia was a part of a 10-year period of semi-obscurity after his conversion, in which he went from Arabia to Damascus, Jerusalem, Syria, and Cilicia (Galatians 1:15–24).[22]

The final dimension of his education was in "Hard Knocks University." In this school, he learned at least two major lessons: (1) he learned how to become all things to all people in order to win some to Christ (1 Corinthians 9:22) and (2) he learned in whatever state he found himself, to be content (Philippians 4:11), or as the NIV states: "I have learned to be content whatever the circumstances." Paul didn't learn those lessons at the synagogue, at Gamaliel's feet, when he got up from the Damascus Road, or even during his years of obscurity. He learned those lessons in his encounters with the Corinthians, Athenians, Galatians, and Ephesians.

He learned great endurance
In troubles, hardships, and distresses;
In beatings, imprisonments, and riots;
In hard work, sleepless nights, and hunger.
From the Holy Spirit, he learned
Sincere love, truthful speech,

And to do his ministry

By the power of God.

(2 Corinthians 6:4–7, NIV, paraphrased)

Paul was a very well-educated man. He had excellent teachers, both human and divine. So who was Paul? He was an unmarried Jewish man (1 Corinthians 7:8), a Roman citizen who spoke Hebrew, Greek, Latin, and Aramaic. He was a highly educated Jewish-Roman-Greek man of his time, who later became a man of God. We have no record of anyone in the first century, who represented Jesus Christ to more people, in more places, with more fervor than the apostle Paul. He was a man *of* the world, who became a man of God *to* the world.

5. Appearance

Neither Luke, Paul, nor any other biblical writer has given us any idea of Paul's appearance. Some of the people of Lystra thought that he was "Hermes," the winged messenger of the gods (Acts 14:12), and some of his enemies in Corinth said his bodily appearance was weak (2 Corinthians 10:10). So we must turn to an extra biblical source called the *Acts of Paul and Thecla*. There, a second century church leader, in the province of Asia, gives this description:

He was a man small of stature,

with a bald head and crooked legs,

in good state of body,

with eye brows meeting

and a nose somewhat hooked,

full of friendliness;

for now he appeared like a man,

and now he had the face of an angel.[23]

6. Ministry and Death

We will devote a later chapter to the ministry of Peter and Paul. We really do not know the time or manner of Paul's death. But tradition says that he, like Peter, died a martyr's death in Rome. Peter was crucified upside down and Paul was beheaded, both on orders from Emperor Nero.[24]

6
Portrait Of Paul:
A Character Sketch

Someone has said that *personality* is who we want people to think we are, *reputation* is what people think we are, and *character* is what we actually are.

After Paul was saved, he was a fanatic for Christ. Read just the first chapter of Philippians, and you'll see a man obsessed with Jesus Christ. He called himself a servant or slave of Christ (1:1), he sends greetings of grace and peace from Christ (1:2), he's confident that Christ will complete his work among the Philippians (1:6), and he longs to see them because of his love for Christ (1:8). The man is "Christ intoxicated." In the KJV, he refers to Jesus Christ no less than 18 times by name—in the first chapter. Doesn't that sound like a fanatic—not according to a scientific or technical definition, but it has a sound of rightness, doesn't it? If it is true, then we must say that by both reputation and character, Paul was first of all a fanatic—both before and after his conversion. Before, he was a fanatic *against* Christ and Christians. Read Luke's description of him in Acts 8:1–3 and 9:1–2. And read Paul's self-description in Acts 22:4; 26:9–11; and Galatians 1:13. Paul used the Greek word translated in the KJV as "zeal." But can you think of a more accurate term than "fanatic"—not necessarily as a negative description, but in the sense of a person who goes all out for what he believes? With such persons, there is no middle ground, no live and let live. One of Paul's character traits was fanaticism.

A second character trait was the desire to *be* right and *do* right. We might call this trait "personal righteousness." Paul declared that as far as the Law was concerned, he was "blameless" (Philippians 3:6, KJV) or "faultless" (NIV). As a Pharisee, he studied the Law and committed himself to keeping it. As a follower of Christ, he came to understand that the Law could not save him; but he did not give up his desire to be righteous. After his conversion, he looked to another source for his righteousness. In his "Letter to the Romans," there is an extensive section, 1:17–6:23, on the matter of being and doing right. Righteousness was not just a part of his theology, but it was a part of his character; it was "in his blood."

A third trait of Paul's character was a "desire for excellence." As a young Pharisee, he advanced in Judaism beyond many Jews of his age. He testified: "I was ahead of most fellow-Jews of my age in my practice of the Jewish religion and was much more devoted to the traditions of our ancestors" (Galatians 1:14). He was striving for excellence. One of the reasons he changed so quickly and dramatically from Judaism to Christ was that he perceived that the knowledge of Christ was more excellent (Philippians 3:8). He was willing to consider all of his Jewish credentials and achievements as "rubbish" because of the excellency of Christ. He turned from the way of the Law to the way of grace, because it was revealed to him that the grace of God in Christ was superior to the Law (Romans 5:20; 6:14; Ephesians 2:8–10). As a Christian, he "approved" love over all of the spiritual gifts because love is "a more excellent way" (1 Corinthians 12:31, KJV). Being excellent was not motivated by outside pressure; it was a part of his inner being, his essence. Paul would have had a special appreciation for this poem on excellence by Douglas Malloch:

> If you can't be a pine on the top of the hill,
>   Be a scrub in the valley—but be
> The best little scrub by the side of the rill,
>   Be a bush if you can't be a tree.
>
> If you can't be a bush be a bit of the grass,
>   And some highway happier make;
> If you can't be a muskie then just be a bass—
>   But the liveliest bass in the lake!
>
> We can't all be captains, we've got to be crew,
>   There's something for all of us here,

There's big work to do, and there's lesser to do,
And the task you must do is the near.

If you can't be a highway then just be a trail,
If you can't be a sun be a star;
It isn't by size that you win or you fail—
Be the best of whatever you are![25]

These traits in no sense exhaust the qualities of Paul's character, but a final trait that we will mention is *vision*. He seemed always to be looking ahead. When he wrote his "Letter to the Philippians," he was believed to be imprisoned in Rome and near the end of his years of ministry. But is he giving up and signing off? No, he's looking forward to getting out of prison and helping the Philippians grow and become happy in their faith (Philippians 1:25). One of his great desires was to preach the Gospel in Rome and, though confined under house arrest, he was free to preach and teach. But his vision was not yet complete. His vision was to carry the Christian message beyond Rome to Spain (Romans 15:24). In fact, his letter sounded like he had planned Rome as just a stop on his way to Spain.

Luke does not tell us that Paul actually went to Spain. He closes his "History" when Paul is still imprisoned in Rome. However, the belief that Paul did eventually travel to Spain is backed up by a sentence in an extra-biblical source, the "Muratorian Fragment," "Paul departed from Rome to Spain."

Paul's ultimate vision was the arrival of the "Day of Christ Jesus" (Philippians 1:6, 10; 2:16). The idea of the coming of the Lord was not original with Paul. It is a vision that was spoken of by Isaiah, Jeremiah, Amos, Micah, and Joel, as well as Peter (2 Peter 3:10, 12) and John (Revelation 6:17; 16:14). It will be a time of joy and reward for the faithful, but a time of condemnation and judgment for the unfaithful and wicked.

Paul was not a normal man. He was a fanatic, a man very much concerned with personal righteousness, devoted to excellence, and always envisioning the future. He was a man used by God to bring Jesus Christ to the first century Roman world.

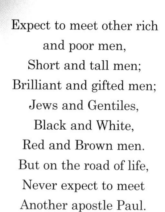

Expect to meet other rich
and poor men,
Short and tall men;
Brilliant and gifted men;
Jews and Gentiles,
Black and White,
Red and Brown men.
But on the road of life,
Never expect to meet
Another apostle Paul.

7
The Ministry Of Peter And Paul

Christian ministry may be defined as Christians helping people who are in need—in the name of Jesus Christ. Jesus said, "For even the Son of man came not to be ministered unto, but to minister, and to give his life a ransom for many" (Mark 10:45, KJV). Jesus was a minister, a servant, a helper, a Person who used His time, His talents, His human and divine gifts, and power for the good of people. Peter described Him as a Person "who went about doing good" (Acts 10:38, KJV).

In the book of Acts, Jesus' work was carried on by His disciples. His two most prominent disciples were Peter and Paul. In this chapter, we want to focus on the ministry of these "two prominent Ps."

I. Sources of Information

The primary sources of information about the ministry of Peter and Paul are Luke's book of Acts and the New Testament letters of Peter and Paul. One of the wonderful things about Luke's "History" is that it fills in some of the gaps and provides background information that supplement and bring to life parts of their letters. Not only can we read Paul's letter to the Philippians, but we can read Acts 16 and discover how the Philippian church was founded and who some of its first members were.

II. Preparation for Ministry

Conversion is the basic preparation for ministry. One has to be a Christian before becoming a Christian minister. No one should attempt to work for the Lord who hasn't met Him, should they? How can we do the Lord's work without the Lord's power? Mission impossible, isn't it?

Peter's preparation for ministry may be thought of in three phases. First was his call to discipleship and years of observing and participating in the ministry of Jesus. Second was his conversion experience. We're not sure when Peter's conversion took place. But we do know that Jesus told him before they went to the Garden of Gethsemane, "when you turn back to me (are converted), you must strengthen your brothers" (Luke 22:32). We know that the Peter we see in Acts is a changed man from the man we saw in the Gospel accounts. The third phase of Peter's preparation for ministry happened when his life was taken over by the Holy Spirit on the Day of Pentecost (Acts 2:1–4). After his pentecostal experience, Peter was possessed by a new boldness and joy, and his actions were characterized by a greater consistency, dependability, and spiritual effectiveness.

Paul's conversion was dramatic and Luke records Paul's conversion story three times in Acts (9:3–9; 22:6–11; 26:12–18). And when Paul refers to it in his Galatian letter (1:11–17), he adds some interesting details about what he did after his conversion. We're glad he made this Galatian reference because the details found there appear nowhere else in the New Testament.

Besides the "physical" details of his conversion, it seems that Paul's conversion convinced him of three things: (1) that he was wrong in his thinking and actions against Christians, (2) that Jesus was alive—rather than being a dead insurrectionist as he had been told (Matthew 28:11–15), and (3) that Jesus had called and appointed Paul to represent Him to the Gentiles. With these three convictions, after a few days with the saints at Damascus, Paul began the first phase of his ministry (Acts 9:20–30).[26]

III. Ministry

A. *Speaking.* We have included under speaking, the ministries of preaching, defending, and teaching. Luke has given us several examples of Peter and Paul's preaching ministry.[27] Examples of Peter's sermons may be found in Acts 2:14–40; 3:12–26; 10:34–43. Two of Paul's sermons are in Acts 13:16–41; 17:22–31. These are probably not their complete sermons—word for word—but the basic message and pattern are preserved. We can see that the sermons were Scripture-based (Old Testament), Christ-centered, and usually called for a response from the hearers.

A second kind of speaking might be called a ministry of defense. The purpose of this apologetic speaking was not to give a salvation message, but to prove that Jesus is the Messiah and that the Christian experience is authentic. Whether these messages were by Peter (4:8–12; 5:29–31), Stephen (7:1–53), or Paul (23:1–6) and whether they were before the Jewish Council, government officials (24:10–21; 26:2–29), or a hostile crowd (22:1–21), the objective was the same. They were attempting to explain who they were as Christians and what their primary beliefs and motives were.

A third kind of speaking was the ministry of teaching. Luke does not give us examples of extended teaching sessions, but he does mention that what we call "Christian education" was a part of the church's ministry. In Acts 2:42, he records that some of the 3,000 new converts "spent their time in learning from the apostles." He also records that an observer reported to the Jewish officials that some of the apostles were "in the Temple teaching the people" (5:25, emphasis added; see also 5:28, 42; 8:26–38). Luke tells us that Barnabas took Paul to Antioch and for a whole year they met "with the people of the church and taught a large group" (11:25–26). For other references to the church's teaching ministry, see 13:12; 16:13–14; 17:1–4, 10–11; 18:4, 11, 26; 19:1–10; 20:31; 28:23–28. Luke closes the book of Acts with these words: "[Paul] preached about the Kingdom of God and taught about the Lord Jesus Christ, speaking with all boldness and freedom" (Acts 28:31).

B. Healing and Miracle Working. To meet needs and to confirm the message of the apostles, the Lord performed healings and other miracles through the apostles. The supreme miracle with which Luke opens his "History" is the resurrection of Jesus, followed by the Ascension (1:2–3, 10–11). The third miracle was the dramatic advent of the Holy Spirit and the anointing of the disciples to speak the Gospel in languages that they did not know (2:1–11).

Scattered throughout Luke's "History" are miraculous healings.

The most well known is found in the third chapter (vv. 1–9) where the Lord healed a lame man through Peter and John. A negative and terrifying miracle of judgment was the death of Ananias and Sapphira. They died trying to deceive the church (5:1–11). Luke closes the story with this comment: "Many miracles and wonders were being performed among the people by the apostles" (5:12). Then he proceeds to tell us in a rather matter-of-fact way that people were healed by Peter's shadow (5:15–16). This would have been amazing had it been Jesus' shadow, but the shadow of formerly cussing, fighting Peter? Truly amazing! We can read of other healings, "great wonders and miracles" through Philip (8:13); through Peter (9:33–42; 12:1–11, 20–23); and through Paul (13:6–12; 14:8–10; 15:12; 16:16–18, 25–31; 19:11–12; 20:7–12). Luke climaxes his "History" with a truly dramatic miracle involving a storm and shipwreck (27:13–44). The dramatic story ends with another miracle on the island of Malta. There Paul survives a snakebite and lives to experience the Lord's healing of the father of Publius, the island's chief (28:1–10).

C. Organizing. Peter and Paul were faced with the challenge of giving structure to the fast-growing group of Christian believers. Within 30 or so years, the church that began with 120 persons in one room on the second floor (Acts 1:13) had grown to several thousand members, and extended throughout much of the Roman Empire. The disciples' first organizational task was replacing Judas, who had betrayed Jesus and committed suicide. Peter helped them face the challenge successfully by leading the group in the selection of Matthias (1:12–26).

A second challenge was baptizing 3,000 (2:41) and later another 2,000 (4:4) converts. Luke doesn't tell us how the apostles did it, but he does tell us how they handled the food distribution crisis by encouraging the believers to select deacons (6:1–6).

Perhaps their most serious challenge was settling the question: How do Gentiles become Christians? One group's answer was: "First they must become Jews" (11:1–3, 15:1). To become a Jew, one must be circumcised and make a commitment to obey all of the Jewish laws, observe the various feasts, and perform the various ceremonies and rituals. A second group said, "No, a person becomes a Christian by believing in Jesus Christ."

The disciples handled this organizational dilemma by calling a meeting to decide the matter. Luke recorded the proceedings and decisions of this meeting in Acts 15:1–35. The decision is summarized in verses 20, 28–30. The way to salvation for a Jew or Gentile is most briefly expressed by Paul in his conversation with the Roman jailer in Philippi, "Believe on the Lord Jesus Christ, and thou shalt be saved" (16:31, KJV).

Luke records a phrase that hints at the setting up of some local church organizational structure. He wrote that Paul and Barnabas went back to Lystra, Iconium, and Antioch of Pisidia and "ordained them elders in every church" (14:23, KJV). This phrase does not seem to apply to all of the newly founded churches, but only those in Lystra, Iconium, Antioch of Pisidia, and perhaps Derbe (14:21). As "headquarters churches," congregations in Jerusalem and Antioch of Syria seem to have been organizationally advanced (see 6:1–7; 9:26–31; 11:1–30; 15:1–35).

D. Evangelizing. Here we are using the terms "evangelist, evangelism, and evangelistic" to describe persons and their Gospel communication activities that took place *outside* of Jerusalem and the cities and towns where the evangelists customarily resided.

> *1. Peter.* Both Peter and Paul were evangelists, as were Philip, Barnabas, Silas, and Timothy. Luke's record of Peter's evangelistic activities is reported in Acts 8, 9, and 10. In chapter 11, Peter reported his Joppa evangelistic experience to the church in Jerusalem (11:5–15).

We feel certain that this was not the full extent of Peter's evangelistic ministry. In Acts 9:32, Luke wrote that "Peter travelled everywhere." Peter addressed his first letter (1 Peter 1:1) to Christian believers in Pontus, Galatia, Cappadocia, Asia, and Bithynia. These were churches he had probably founded or visited. Although it is often disputed, Roman Catholic tradition describes Peter as the possible founder of the church in Rome and its first bishop. The fact that Peter *preached* in Rome, aside from Roman Catholic tradition, is accepted as true by many Bible scholars and students.

> *2. Paul.* Luke leaves no doubt that the most outstanding evangelist of the early church was Paul. He is described as doing some evangelistic work in Damascus a "few days" after his dramatic conversion (Acts 9:19–26). Later he "went all over Jerusalem, preaching boldly . . . . He also talked and disputed with the Greek-speaking Jews" (9:28–29). When these Jews tried to kill him, the believers whisked him out of town to Caesarea and sent him back home to Tarsus (9:30).

Luke uses most of the rest of his book to describe Paul's evangelistic activities—beginning in Antioch and ending in Rome (Acts 28:14). Luke focuses his report on three evangelistic campaigns, usually referred to as "Paul's missionary journeys" (13:4–14:28; 15:36–18:22; 18:23–21:16). Sit down and read about these campaigns. You'll smile, you'll cry, you'll praise God, and you'll ask, "How could the Lord let that happen?" You'll wonder sometimes if Paul is going to make it to Rome and you'll shout a tearful "Hallelujah!" when he finally does. If you can part with the beloved King James Version, read the "adventures of the evangelist tours" in another version or translation, such as the *New International Version* (NIV). Reading Luke's action-packed report of Paul's evangelistic tours can be a truly thrilling experience. For a simple, organized presentation of Paul's missionary journeys, read *Exploring the New Testament.*[28]

E. Fund-Raising. Another important part of ministry in the first century church, as in our present churches, was fund-raising. In Acts, the first recorded need for special funds took place shortly after Pentecost. The situation was taken care of when believers shared what they had with each other. The next step was taken when those who had "property and possessions" sold it and the apostles distributed the money to those in need (2:44–45; 4:34–37).

A third step was taken when seven deacons were selected and given the specific responsibility of handling finances and making sure that everyone received what they needed (6:1–6). Later Dorcas was cited for using her sewing skills to minister to widows in her community (9:36–39). From the church in Antioch of Syria, Paul and Barnabas carried money to Jerusalem to those adversely affected by a famine. This was the severe famine that Agabus predicted (11:27–30; see also 2 Corinthians 8:1–15; 9:1–15). One of the purposes of Paul's letter to the Philippians was to thank them for their generosity to him (Philippians 2:30; 4:10–19). It was while urging the elders of Ephesus to "help the weak" that Paul revealed some words of Jesus that might have gone unrecorded: "Remember the words of the Lord Jesus, how he said, "It is more blessed to give than to receive" (Acts 20:35, KJV).

F. Writing. A final ministry of both Peter and Paul was the ministry of communicating through the written word. We probably do not have all of the literature that was written by either Peter or Paul. But the literature that we do possess is very important and precious. Of Peter's writings, we only have two letters (1 and 2 Peter), and from Paul's pen only 13 or 14 letters, depending on whether or not Paul wrote Hebrews. Strictly speaking, Peter and Paul's writing ministry is not a part of Luke's portrait, but we're including them here as an acknowledgment of writing as a ministry and as a challenge to those whom the Lord may be impressing to sit down and "stir up the [writing] gift" that is within them (2 Timothy 1:6, KJV).

Peter wrote his first letter to encourage the readers who were facing persecution and suffering for their faith. His second letter was written to combat false teaching and the immorality that results from such teaching. There is still great need for Christian encouragement and teaching literature, isn't there? Is there a need for Christian literature written by African American Christians?

Paul wrote letters that can be classified into three categories:

1. Eight letters to churches
   Colossians
   Corinthians (2)
   Ephesians
   Thessalonians (2)
   Philippians
   Romans

2. Four letters to individuals
   Philemon
   Timothy (2)
   Titus

3. Two letters to Christians in various locations
   Hebrews (?)
   Galatians

Had not Peter and Paul exercised their writing ministry, both the church of the first century, our century, and centuries to come would be much poorer in mind and spirit.

Whether speaking, healing, organizing, evangelizing, fund-raising, or writing, Peter, Paul, and other believers of the early church are portrayed by Luke as persons empowered by the Holy Spirit to minister to the needs of people in Jesus' name.

8
Other Prominent Persons In Acts

We do not mean to imply that Peter and Paul are the only important persons in Acts or that they did all or most of the ministry. They are the persons that Luke featured most prominently, but just as a leader cannot lead effectively today without followers and faithful and capable assistants, so the early church needed capable and committed people to help the church move forward.

Barnabas

One of the important persons in a supporting role was Barnabas. His name means "One who Encourages" (4:36). Luke mentioned him often and characterized him as "a good man, full of the Holy Spirit and faith" (11:24). He was a Levite from Cyprus, and the uncle of John Mark who wrote one of the accounts of Jesus' life. Barnabas was known for his generosity (4:36–37) and was Paul's companion on their first evangelistic tour (13:2).

Stephen

Another important person was Stephen, the preaching deacon. We do not know much about Stephen. We don't know when or where he was born, or who his parents were. But we know he was a "full" man. Luke said he was *"full* of faith and the Holy Spirit" (6:5, emphasis added). He also said that Stephen was a man richly blessed by God, who being *full* of power "performed great miracles and wonders among the people" (6:8). From his sermon recorded by Luke in Acts 7, we know he was full of Scripture and was so full of love that he forgave his enemies as they stoned him to death (7:60).

Philip

Philip was also a preaching deacon (6:5) through whom God

worked miracles of physical and spiritual healing (8:5–7). When Philip preached "the Good News of the Kingdom of God and about Jesus Christ," both men and women believed and were baptized (8:12). And Luke made a special note of the "great joy" that came to the city (8:8). We must give God special thanks for Philip. He obeyed the Holy Spirit and was the instrument God used to send the Gospel message to our ancestors in Ethiopia, Africa (8:26–39).

Dorcas

Undoubtedly one of the most appreciated women in Acts was Dorcas (Greek) or Tabitha (Hebrew). She was loved because she was a woman of love. Luke said, "She spent all her time doing good and helping the poor" (9:36). When she died, the believers sent for Peter, who called her back to life and presented her to the widows and other believers to whom she had demonstrated her love by sewing shirts and coats for them (9:36–41). Luke said that as a result of her new life, "many people believed in the Lord" (9:42).

Ananias

What might have happened to Paul if Ananias had not been obedient to the Lord in his vision (9:10)? What a wonderful little drama of faith in action!

The Lord:	"Ananias"
Ananias:	"Here I am."
The Lord:	"Go to Saul. I have chosen Saul for a special task."
Response:	So Ananias went . . . .

We hear no more about Ananias, except in Paul's testimony of his conversion (22:12). This man came on the scene at just the right time, fulfilled his purpose, and disappeared from view. But for every person won to Christ by Paul's evangelistic efforts and his writings, guess who got a "credit mark" in God's record book? Yes, Ananias!

(Now, this is not the Ananias of the tragic Ananias-Sapphira, husband-wife team in Acts 5:1–11. That Ananais and his wife died "in church" and were buried without a funeral.)

Silas

We first hear about Silas as being a delegate to the Jerusalem Council (15:1–21). The meeting was called to decide how Gentiles could become Christians. When the decision was made that everybody, both Jews and Gentiles, is saved by God's grace (15:11), Silas was chosen as one of the men to carry the Apostolic Letter to churches in various locations outside of Jerusalem (15:22). Luke noted that Silas was a highly respected prophet (15:22, 27, 32). In fact, he was held in such high esteem that Paul chose him as his partner for his second evangelistic tour (15:40). Perhaps Silas is most famous as the man who could sing and pray at midnight after being severely beaten and thrown into a Philippian dungeon (16:22–25). Even after this painful incident, Silas continued with Paul to Thessalonica, Berea, and Corinth. It seems that Silas also traveled and assisted Peter, who regarded him as "a faithful [Christian] brother" (1 Peter 5:12, KJV).

Lydia

A fitting title for Lydia would be "Sister Hospitality." Lydia was a beautiful, intelligent Jewish businesswoman, who worshiped the Lord out under the sky (Acts 16:14). When she heard about Jesus, she believed and with her household was baptized. She asked Paul, Silas, and Luke, "Come and stay in my house . . . " (16:15). Apparently her house became their headquarters. When they were released from jail, they went back to her house, encouraged the little new assembly, and went on their way. Perhaps Lydia had gone home to be with the Lord by the time Paul wrote his Philippian letter. Surely he would have sent his personal greetings to this lady of hospitality.

This short list in no sense exhausts the roll call of those who played "assistant roles" in Luke's "History." These are simply the most prominent. Only the Lord knows the complete list of those whose faithfulness caused the Word of the Lord to keep "spreading and growing stronger" (19:20).

PART III
Luke's Portrait Of
The Early Church

In Part I, we looked at the book of Acts and Luke, its author. Part II focused on prominent individuals in the early church. In Part III, we want to answer the question: What are some of the outstanding characteristics of the early Christian Church as portrayed by Luke in the book of Acts? There seem to be at least five. The church was Christ-directed and Spirit-empowered; it was a worshiping, ministering, and expanding church. In the final chapter, we want to reflect on the first century Church as a model for the African American Christian Church. Are there some mistakes we can avoid? What are some things we can do to help bring about positive changes in our communities and cities, as the first century Church did in their communities and cities? How can we allow Christ to direct us and the Spirit to empower us so that our people are made healthier, holier, happier, more helpful, and productive? Those are the kinds of questions we want to explore in the final chapter.

9

The Christ-Directed Church

Tell me the story of Jesus,
Write on my heart every word.
Tell me the story most precious,
Sweetest that ever was heard.[29]

Fanny Crosby (1820–1915)

Are these statements true or false?

_____1. Acts is primarily about the work of the Holy Spirit.

_____2. Acts is primarily about the work of the Holy Spirit through the apostles.

_____3. Acts is primarily Luke's account of the ministry of Peter and Paul.

_____4. Acts is primarily the story of how the Holy Spirit "took over" Jesus' work after His ascension.

If you answered "false" to all of the statements, your grade is A+. The book of Acts is about the work of the Holy Spirit. It is about Peter and Paul, but it is primarily about Jesus Christ! It is Luke's account about: (1) how Jesus Christ challenged His 11 disciples to go back to Jerusalem and wait for His power, (2) how *Jesus Christ* sent the Holy Spirit to fill or fully control the disciples and other believers, (3) how Jesus' Spirit anointed Peter, Stephen, Philip, Paul, and others to witness about Him from Jerusalem to Rome, and (4) how their witnessing about *Jesus Christ* formed a movement called the Church of *Jesus Christ*. As a result of this First Century Movement, Jesus Christ now has over one billion followers on planet Earth. Luke's purpose in Acts was the same as his purpose in his Gospel account—to tell the story of Jesus.

1. Jesus Christ: Founder of the Church

Jesus told the disciples of His plan on their leadership retreat in Caesarea Philippi. After asking who they thought He was and receiving God's answer through Peter, Jesus promised that He would build His church and that nothing would be able to destroy it (Matthew 16:13–20).

Did His disciples believe Him? Was the idea crushed in their minds by His betrayal, suffering, and crucifixion? Whatever they believed before and after His death was altered by His resurrection, His 40 days of fellowship with them, and His ascension. How was He going to build a church now that He has gone to heaven? The answer was that His *body* was gone, but His Spirit was *present*. Before He had been with them, now through His Spirit He was going to be in them (John 14:17). So He told them to go back to Jerusalem and wait until they became unmistakably aware of His presence and power. When that happened, they would become witnesses for Him in Jerusalem, Judea, Samaria, and "to the ends of the earth" (Acts 1:8).

When they began witnessing for Him, the church He told them about earlier came into being with Jesus Christ as its founder and Peter as its first visible leader (Matthew 16:18–19; Acts 2:14; 3:4–8, 12; 4:8; 5:3, 9, 15, 29; 9:32–11:18; 12:3–19).

2. Jesus Christ: Center of the Church

Reading through Luke's "History," 21st century Christians are struck by the number and prominence of Old Testament references. The Old Testament was all the Scripture the early believers had. But we are struck also by how they used these Scriptures as the basis of their witness about Jesus. Every sermon and testimony in Acts is about Jesus Christ. In Peter's first sermon on Pentecost Sunday (Acts 2:21), he quoted a five-verse passage from Joel (2:28–32). Then he said, "Listen to these words, fellow-Israelites! *Jesus of Nazareth* was a man whose divine authority was clearly proven . . ." (Acts 2:22, emphasis added). Later in his sermon he quoted David (Psalm 16:8–11; 132:11; 110:1), and applied David's words to the resurrection (Acts 2:31) and ascension of Jesus the Messiah (2:35). Peter declared that the One the Jews had crucified, God had made "Lord and Messiah" (2:36) and that they should be baptized in His name (2:38).

When Stephen gave his witness, he began with a sketch of

Israel's history beginning with Abraham, through Moses, Joshua, David, and Solomon to Isaiah. But the climax of his sermon was his accusation that his listeners had killed God's "righteous Servant" (7:52), Jesus Christ. He said, "And now you have betrayed and murdered *him*" (7:52, emphasis added). It was for Stephen's preaching about Jesus that he was assassinated; and it was Jesus whom he saw standing to receive him into heaven. He asked Jesus to forgive his murderers and committed his spirit into Jesus' hands as they stoned him to death (7:59–60).

When we study the sermon of Philip in Samaria, we discover him preaching "the Good News of the Kingdom of God and about *Jesus Christ*" (8:12, emphasis added). When he witnessed to the African administrator, "he told him the Good News about *Jesus*" (8:35, emphasis added).

When Saul was struck down on the Damascus Road and asked who was responsible; the answer came, "I am *Jesus,* whom you persecute" (9:5, emphasis added). It was Jesus Christ who gave Saul his assignment (9:15–16) and when he began his witness, he preached that "*Jesus* was the Son of God . . . . the Messiah" (9:20, 22, emphasis added). When Peter preached to Cornelius, his family, and guests, he preached about "the Good News of peace through *Jesus Christ*" (10:36, emphasis added) and about the death and resurrection of Jesus Christ, through whom forgiveness is available "through the power of his name" (10:39–43).

When Paul, Barnabas, Silas, and others went on their evangelistic tours, the heart of their message was about *Jesus Christ.* Whether in Antioch of Pisidia (13:23–39), Derbe (14:21), Philippi (16:30–31), Thessalonica (17:3), Athens (17:31), Corinth (18:5), Ephesus (18:28; 19:4–5), or finally in Rome, it can be said of the first century Christian witnesses, as Luke said of Paul: "He preached about the Kingdom of God and taught about the *Lord Jesus Christ,* speaking with all boldness . . ." (28:31, emphasis added).

In Acts, as in the Gospel accounts, Jesus Christ is the central figure, the main character, the church's primary focus. In His name and by His power people were forgiven, baptized into the church, healed, helped, and radically changed. In Acts, Jesus Christ is the center of the church's life, witness, teaching, and worship.

3. Jesus Christ: Director of the Church

"You will be witnesses for me in Jerusalem, in all of Judea and Samaria, and to the ends of the earth" (Acts 1:8).

As founder and center of the Church, Jesus is also the Church's leader and chief administrator. Jesus told His disciples where He wanted the church to start and the path along which He wanted it to move forward. He said, "in Jerusalem" (1:8), the disciples' religious hometown and the center of Jewish history and worship (Acts 1:12–8:1). They were then to witness to people in Judea, the region or "state" in which Jerusalem was located (Acts 8:1, 40; 9:1, 32–43). Next Jesus directed them to the Samaritans, the outcasts, the despised people who were part Jew and part Gentile (8:1, 4–25). From Jerusalem, Judea, and Samaria, they were to expand their ministry to all the world. This "to all the world" command was spearheaded by Paul and those who accompanied him (Acts 13:1–14:28; 15:36–21:16; 28:1–31).

This expansion sounds so logical, but Jesus' plan was not carried out by simple logic. When Paul and Silas had witnessed in the regions of Phrygia and Galatia, the next logical step was to proceed into Asia and Bithynia, but "the Spirit of Jesus did not allow them" (16:6–7, NRSV). Jesus did not let them go into this region because He had plans at the time for them to go to Philippi (16:11–40). Paul did not insist on going to Asia and Bithynia because he knew who was in charge of the missionary journey. He listened to his Leader and obeyed His directions. From the beginning of Paul's entrance into the Church, he never doubted that Jesus was its founder, center, and director.

Earlier when Philip was carrying on a great revival in Samaria, the Lord sent an angel to tell him to leave the revival crowds and go to the desert to speak to one Black brother (8:26ff.). Now, that's not logical, is it—to leave hundreds of people to minister to one minority brother from a foreign country? Well, Philip didn't argue because he knew who was in charge. So he went as he was directed, led the brother to Jesus Christ, baptized him, and was called away to his next place of service (8:26–40).

Have we made the point? The book of Acts is about Jesus Christ, who is the founder, center, and director of the Church. The early Christian Church was Christ-directed.

10
A Spirit-Empowered Church

In one sense, this is a rather difficult chapter to write because Luke was not a professional theologian, and in no sense attempted a systematic presentation of the Person and work of the Holy Spirit. Acts contains at least 61 references (KJV) to the Holy Spirit, and Luke speaks of Him in at least 21 different ways.

Purpose

It is not our purpose in this chapter to attempt to develop a doctrine of the Holy Spirit from Luke's "History" or to impose a doctrine on his book. Neither is it our purpose to set forth or defend the perspective of any particular person or denomination. Our purpose is to look at Luke's story of the early Christian Church and to determine how he perceived the Holy Spirit in the first century context. We will achieve our purpose by asking and attempting to answer two questions:

1. What did Luke write about the Holy Spirit?
2. What did Luke show to be the relationship between the Holy Spirit and the early Christian Church?

I. What did Luke write about the Holy Spirit?

A. Names: In the Bible, the Holy Spirit is called by many names. In the Old Testament, He is sometimes called (KJV): "the Spirit of God" (Genesis 1:2), "the Spirit of the LORD" (Judges 14:6, 19; 15:14), the "holy spirit" (Psalm 51:11; Isaiah 63:10, 11), and simply the "spirit" (Psalm 139:7). In the New Testament, He is sometimes called: "the Spirit" (Matthew 4:1; Mark 1:10, 12), the "Comforter" (John 14:16, KJV), "the Spirit of truth" (John 15:26, KJV), the "Spirit of life" (Romans 8:2, KJV), "the Spirit of Christ" (Romans 8:9), and "the Spirit of adoption" (Romans 8:15, KJV).

In Luke's Gospel account, he refers to the Holy Spirit as: (1) "the Holy Ghost" (Luke 1:35; 4:1, KJV), (2) "the Spirit of the Lord" (Luke 4:18), and (3) "the Holy Spirit" (Luke 11:13). In the book of Acts, Luke refers to the Spirit in three ways primarily: the Holy Spirit (43 times), the Spirit (eight times), and the Gift (five times). Secondarily he refers to the Holy Spirit as: the Lord's Spirit (one time), the Spirit of the Lord (one time), the Spirit of Jesus (one time), and the power of the Spirit (two times).

B. Roles: Luke portrays the Holy Spirit as being so active in the book of Acts that someone has suggested that Luke's "History" should be called "The Gospel of the Holy Spirit" or "The Acts of the Holy Spirit."[30] Let's look at a summary list of Luke's portrayal of the Spirit's active and passive roles.

    1. Active Roles

      a) The Holy Spirit fills or fully controls believers: 13 references.

      b) The Holy Spirit gives believers additional spiritual qualities such as wisdom (three times), faith (two times), power (one time), and joy (one time): seven references.

      c) The Holy Spirit baptizes (two times), empowers (six times), and helps believers (two times): 10 references.

      d) The Holy Spirit speaks to (four times) and through (three times) believers: seven ref ences.

      e) The Holy Spirit rebukes (one time), warns (one time), and forbids (one time): three references.

      f) The Holy Spirit sets believers apart (one time), gives them leadership tasks (one time), sends and takes them on assignments (two times), and assigns people to care for leaders (one time): five references.

    2. Passive Roles

      a) The Holy Spirit is poured out (six times) or comes down (two times) on believers: eight references.

    b) The Holy Spirit is given to (two times), received by (six times), and is present with (one time), believers: nine references.

    c) The Holy Spirit is lied to (one time), tested (one time), or resisted (one time): three references.

    d) The Holy Spirit is agreed with (two times) and obeyed by (one time) believers: three references.

Summary: In the book of Acts, Luke portrays the Spirit 45 times as active and 23 times as passive.

II. What did Luke show to be the relationship between the Holy Spirit and the early Christian Church?

A. The Holy Spirit related itself to the Church's leaders, who were carrying out Jesus' instructions. He was active in the ministries of Peter (4:8; 8:15–17; 10:19, 47; 11:12, 15; 15:8), Stephen (6:5, 10; 7:55), Philip (8:29, 39), Ananias (9:17), Barnabas (11:24; 13:2, 4), and Paul (13:9; 16:6–7; 19:6; 20:22–23; 28:25).

B. The Holy Spirit related itself to the Church generally (2:17, 38; 4:31; 6:3; 8:15–18; 9:31; 13:52; 15:28; 19:2, 6; 20:28; 21:4).

C. The Holy Spirit related itself to Gentiles who became the Church's largest group of constituents (8:15–18, 29; 10:44–47; 13:52; 15:8; 19:2–6).

D. The Holy Spirit (occasionally) related itself to nonbelievers and believers who were unfaithful. Two unfortunate examples are Ananias and Sapphira (5:1–11, 3 and 9) and Elymas, the magician (13:6–12, 9–11).

E. Luke does not spell out the relationship between the Holy Spirit and the Word in bold letters, but he seems to make a quiet, tacit, understated connection between the Spirit and the Word—especially as it relates to the expansion of the Church. One of the underlying themes is that the Word of God was proclaimed, and the Church grew because believers were directed by Jesus and empowered by His Spirit (see 2:41, 47; 4:31; 5:14; 6:7; 8:12).

One of Luke's progress reports is found in Acts 9:31: "And so it was that the church throughout Judea, Galilee, and Samaria had a time of peace. Through the help of the Holy Spirit it was strengthened and grew in numbers, as it lived in reverence for the Lord."

11
A Worshiping Church

Worship is realizing the presence and power of God and responding by consciously adjusting our wills to His will. Worship is experienced when that which is deepest within us reaches up to God in adoration, confession, thanksgiving, petition, and commitment. If a new, dramatic, and dynamic consciousness of the Holy Spirit signaled the birth of the Church, then the Church was actually born during worship. Earlier, Jesus told Sister Samaritan (the woman at the well), that God was looking for people—sincere, spiritual people—to worship Him (John 4:23, KJV). In the early Christian Church, God found some of those people.

1. Times. At first the Church did not worship on Sunday at 11:00 a.m. and on Wednesday at 6:45 p.m. as many churches do today. Neither did they worship only on Sunday, Tuesday, and Friday as some other churches do, nor on Saturday as some Christians do. When the Christian Church began, Luke wrote that they met "frequently" (Acts 1:14). Sometimes they met in the morning, before 9:00 a.m. (2:15), or "day after day" (2:46), or at 3:00 p.m. (3:1). They sometimes met for several hours (5:7), and sometimes they met every day (5:42).

2. Places. There were no cathedrals with plush cushioned pews, no stained glass windows and mighty pipe organs. There were no air-conditioned sanctuaries with beautiful pulpit furniture, wonderfully robed choirs and state-of-the-art educational facilities. In fact, there weren't even any storefront churches lined up side by side with different denominational labels. There were mainly just people who got together for worship and fellowship. Sometimes they gathered in a second story room (1:13), at the temple (2:46; 3:1), and in each other's homes (2:46; 12:12). Outside of Jerusalem, Paul frequently met for worship in Jewish synagogues (17:10, 17; 18:4). He also met down by the riverside (16:13), and he and Silas worshiped in prison (16:25). In Rome, he held worship services in his rented house or apartment (28:30–31).

3. Prayer. It seems that early church believers worshiped wherever they wanted to or needed to. One of the components of their worship was prayer. Luke portrays the early Christian Church as a praying church. In Luke's Gospel account—Jesus' final recorded act, before His ascension—was prayer. "He raised his hands and blessed them" (Luke 24:50). And after the disciples walked the six blocks (a Sabbath Day's journey) back to Jerusalem, Luke writes, "They gathered frequently to pray" (Acts 1:14). When they were trying to choose a 12th disciple to take Judas's place, "they prayed" (1:24). When they gathered for teaching, fellowship, and eating, they prayed (2:42) and praised God (2:47). When the lame man was healed, Peter and John were on their way to the temple to pray (3:1) and when the man was healed, he and the people who saw him broke out in praise (3:8–9). When Peter and John returned from their meeting with the Jewish Council, the believers "all joined together in prayer" (4:24). The prayer was so beautiful and powerful that Luke recorded it (4:24–30). Deacons were chosen so that the apostles could give their "full time to prayer and the work of preaching" (6:4). The deacons were then consecrated to their task by prayer and the laying on of the apostles' hands (6:6). Stephen, one of the preaching deacons and the first recorded Christian to die for his faith, died praying for those who stoned him (7:59–60). "Lord Jesus, receive my spirit!" he said (7:59). "He knelt down and cried out in a loud voice, 'Lord! Do not remember this sin against them!' He said this and died" (v. 60).

In Samaria, the apostles prayed for the Samaritan believers to receive the Holy Spirit (8:15) and told Simon to repent and pray to be forgiven for thinking he could buy miracle-working power (8:22). On the Damascus Road, as soon as Saul was convinced that he was actually talking to Jesus, he prayed a prayer of surrender: "What shall I do, Lord?" (22:10). The Lord directed him to Ananias, who had already been praying (9:10–16), and was told that Saul was now praying (9:11).

> How was Dorcas brought back to life (9:40)?
>
> How did Peter and Cornelius meet each other (10:2–9)?
>
> How was Peter set free from prison (12:6, 12)?
>
> How were Paul and Barnabas chosen and sent on their evangelistic tour (13:3)?

"Prayer" is the answer to each question. Shall we speak of prayer in Philippi (16:13, 16, 25), the prayer-hug in Troas (20:10), or the prayer of ignorance in Ephesus (19:11–16)? Shall we recall the tearful prayer of resignation in Ptolemais (21:14)? Or the prayer in court for Agrippa (26:29)? On Paul's journey to Rome, Luke records that there was prayer at sea, prayer on the island of Malta, and prayer outside of Rome (27:23–24; 28:8, 15). From the first to the last chapter of his "History," Luke pictures the church in prayer.

4. Scripture. Can you imagine coming to church for worship and hearing no Scripture read, recited, taught, or preached? The use of Scripture in worship is not an original addition to our modern church worship services. In fact, it was not original with the first century church. It began at least as far back as the Ten Commandments. God wrote the Commandments as the first Scripture (Deuteronomy 5:22) and when Moses broke the tablets, God wrote them again (Deuteronomy 10:4) and told Moses to teach them to the people and for the adults to teach them to their children (Deuteronomy 5:31; 6:7–9).

The Scriptures eventually included the books of Moses (Genesis–Deuteronomy), the Books of the Prophets, the Psalms, and what we now call the Books of Poetry (Job–Song of Solomon). By the time of Jesus, the Scriptures consisted of what we now call the Old Testament. The Old Testament Scriptures were the Bible of the early Christian Church. Later some of the letters of Paul were added, along with the Gospel accounts and the Acts of the Apostles. But the early church had only the Old Testament. Let's see how Luke portrays their use of Old Testament Scripture in worship and witness.

They were familiar with Scripture. Luke is not a preacher and therefore does not usually use his voice to make direct dogmatic statements. He is an artist, a storyteller, and dramatist. He presents his characters and makes inferences from which we are to draw implications. There are two inferences that jump off the pages at us. The first is that the early Christian leaders were very familiar with Old Testament Scriptures. Luke records over 100 references to Old Testament Scripture verses, persons, and events. Second, Luke's record shows a basic unity in the way the early church leaders use Scripture.

They used Scripture among the Jews. The way Scripture is used in Acts depends on what person or group is being addressed. It depends on whether the group is Jewish or Gentile. Among Jews and Jewish Christians, the Scripture is used in four primary ways:

> To show events as fulfilled prophecy
> To provide guidance for action
> To prove Jesus was the Messiah
> To provide a basis for the Gentiles' evangelism

There was certainly some overlapping, but these are four distinct ways that early church leaders used Scripture.

To show events as fulfilled prophecy. When the disciples got back to Jerusalem, the first order of business was to replace Judas. Peter began to address the group by saying, "My fellow-believers . . . the *scripture* had to come true" (Acts 1:16, emphasis added), and then he went on to quote David's prediction about Judas (1:16–20; Psalm 69:25). Peter did the same thing when trying to explain to the Jews what was happening on the Day of Pentecost (Acts 2:16–21; Joel 2:28–32), and by what power the man was healed at the Beautiful Gate (Acts 4:11; Psalm 118:22).

To provide guidance for action. Peter used *Scripture* to suggest that someone should take Judas's place of service (Acts 1:20; Psalm 109:8). A similar use of Scripture was made by James in reference to rules regarding Gentiles as converts (Acts 15). The decision was to instruct the Gentiles to observe some very basic laws laid down by Moses in Exodus 34:15–17 and Leviticus 17:10–16; 18:6–23. When Paul decided to shave his head and observe certain purification procedures (Acts 18:18; 21:23–24), the decision was based on Numbers 6:13–21.

To prove Jesus was the Messiah. This was by far the most frequent use of Scripture. This was one of the early church's greatest challenges when encountering their fellow Jews. The Jews generally, including the disciples, were looking for a conquering, kingdom restoring, powerful Messiah like David. And even after Jesus' resurrection, their basic question was: "Lord, will you at this time give the Kingdom back to Israel?" (Acts 1:6).

For much of their history, the Jewish people had been oppressed. Their time of greatest freedom and glory was under the leadership of David and his son Solomon. So the question on many Jews minds was, "When are we going to be free again, in charge of our own land and destiny?" Now Jesus told them He was not that kind of Messiah but that He had to suffer and establish an inner spiritual kingdom. He said, "My kingdom is not of this world" (John 18:36, KJV). But their need for freedom was so deeply felt that they couldn't hear Jesus. And it was only after Pentecost that the Spirit convinced them that in spite of, in fact, *because of* His suffering, Jesus was indeed the Messiah. Now their challenge was to convince their fellow Jews of this Spirit-revealed truth. One of the ways they tried to do it was by the use of Scripture. If you would like to see how they did it, review these references:

Acts	Old Testament Reference
2:24–30	Psalm 16:8–11; 132:11
2:34–35	2 Samuel 7:12–13
3:18–22	Psalm 110:1
26:22–23	Deuteronomy 18:15, 18
	Isaiah 42:6; 49:6

To provide a basis for the Gentiles' evangelism. In addition to proving that Jesus was the Messiah, some Jewish Christians had to justify carrying the message of salvation to the Gentiles and accepting them as members of the Christian Church. They had to overcome the Jewish idea that they and they alone were "God's chosen people" and that all other people were "dogs" (Mark 7:27–28). Now there was a Jewish way to rise above one's "dog status." It was by becoming a Jewish proselyte; that is, by being circumcised and obeying the Jewish laws, customs, and rituals. Persons such as Philip, Peter, and Paul began to preach to the Gentiles, who began to accept Jesus as Saviour. Then the big discussion in the early church became: Shall we insist that Gentiles become Jews before we accept them as Christians? Luke records two meetings at which the question was discussed. In Acts 2, the Gentiles are accepted because under Peter's ministry they received the gift of the Spirit. Luke writes that when the Jerusalem believers heard that "God gave those Gentiles the same gift . . . they stopped their criticism and praised God . . ." (11:17–18).

In Acts 15, Luke gives us a summary of the second, more inclusive meeting, usually referred to as the Jerusalem Conference. The decision at this meeting was based on Scripture and the reports of Paul, Barnabas, and Peter. There were probably others who spoke, some "pro" and some "con." We know that Judas, Barnabas, and Silas were present (15:22). In his summation, James, the brother of Jesus, quoted Amos 9:11–12 as scriptural support for Gentiles' inclusion and referred to Exodus 34:15; Leviticus 17:10–16; 18:6–23.

The final Scripture quoted in Luke's "History" is Isaiah 6:9–10. Paul applied this Scripture to the Jews in Rome, who refused to believe that Jesus was their Messiah, even after Paul had talked with them from "morning till night" (Acts 28:23, 25). Some believed when he quoted "from the Law of Moses and the writings of the prophets" (28:23). To the others he said, "'How well the Holy Spirit spoke through the prophet Isaiah to your ancestors!' For he said, 'Go and say to this people: You will listen and listen, but not understand; you will look and look, but not see, because this people's minds are dull, and they have stopped up their ears and closed their eyes. Otherwise, their eyes would see, their ears would hear, their minds would understand, and they would turn to me, says God, And I would heal them'" (28:25–27).

When he finished this quote, he concluded: "You are to know, then, that God's message of salvation has been sent to the Gentiles. They will listen!" (28:28)

In at least these four ways, Jewish Christian leaders used Scripture when communicating with Christian and non-Christian Jews. But how did Christian leaders use Scripture among the Gentiles?

They used Scripture among Gentiles. Luke records the use of Scripture among Gentiles in three primary ways:

> To provide historical background for an understanding of Jewish people, events and practices

> To show the connection between Jesus and the Jewish religion

> To illustrate the relationship between the Jewish and non-Jewish understanding of God

As we read through Acts, we notice that the farther we move away from Jerusalem, the fewer Old Testament references we find. Have you noticed that? It's like preaching to African Americans. The further away we move from Atlanta, Georgia, and Montgomery, Birmingham, and Selma, Alabama, the less effective the quotations are from Martin Luther King Jr. and other southern Civil Rights leaders. However, let's look at the way Christians used Scripture among Gentiles.

To provide historical background. As Paul, Peter, and others moved farther away from Judea, the less meaningful they knew quotes from the Jewish Bible would be. But they still used some Scriptures to help Gentile people understand who the Jews were and to explain certain Jewish people, events, and practices. Two examples are Peter with Cornelius (Acts 10:34; see also Deuteronomy 10:17), and Paul speaking before Felix and Agrippa. Before Felix, he referred to the

Laws of Moses and the Books of the Prophets, as well as to sacritices offered in the temple and to ceremonies of purification (Acts 24:14, 18). And before Agrippa, he referred to the "twelve tribes" (26:6–7), but he made no direct scriptural quotations. Felix was knowledgeable about Christianity (24:22) and Agrippa was said to be an expert in Judaism (26:26), but Paul realized that as far as their practical relationship to God was concerned, they were basically pagan Roman politicians. Quoting a lot of Scripture verses would have been an exercise in futility. Paul gave enough historical background to support his testimony and a subtle presentation of the Gospel.

To show the Jesus–Jewish connection. A second way that Christian leaders used the Scriptures was to show how Jesus "fitted into" the Jewish religion. Judaism was one of many religions allowed to coexist in the Roman Empire. It had been in existence for many years before the Roman Empire came into being and as long as it was practiced peacefully, it was allowed its place. Christianity was new, brand-new, and was violently opposed by Jews throughout the Empire. A task of Christians was to identify Christ and His followers with Judaism and to show that Christianity was really what God meant Judaism to be. Even though he was in Jerusalem speaking to Jews, isn't that what Stephen was trying to say (Acts 7)? In his attempt, he used no less that 55 references from 11 Old Testament books. Isn't that also an underlying theme of Paul's presentation in Antioch of Pisidia (13:16–41)? There he quotes from Numbers 14:34; Deuteronomy 1:31; Psalm 2:7; 16:10; Habakkuk 1:5. By name he mentions Abraham, Moses, Samuel, Saul, and David. Paul was in a Gentile city, speaking in a synagogue to both Jews and Gentiles (Acts 13:16, 26). As usual, the Gentiles were more receptive to his message than the Jews (13:47–48).

To bridge the gap between the Jewish and non-Jewish understanding of God. Perhaps Luke's two most effective examples of this use of Scripture are Paul's presentations at Lystra (14:8–21) and Athens (17:16–31). In Lystra, Luke does not report that Paul quoted any Scripture directly. Instead he talked about "the living God, who made heaven, earth, sea, and all that is in them" (14:15; an allusion to Exodus 20:11). Paul asserted that this "living God" is the same

God that gives "rain from heaven and crops at the right times" (Acts 14:17; alluding to Psalm 146:6–7). It seems that Paul is alluding to Scripture here to make a connection between the Greek gods, Zeus and Hermes (Acts 14:11–13), and the "living God" of Jews and Christians. He used the same approach in Athens with the Epicureans, Stoics, and city council members. He discovered a statue "To an Unknown God" (17:23), and used it to introduce his hearers to the Jewish-Christian "God, who made the world and everything in it, the Lord of heaven and earth" (17:24). It seems that Paul did not attempt to make the Athenians aware of Scripture, but he used his knowledge of the Scriptures (1 Kings 8:27; Isaiah 42:5) and of their poets, whom he quoted, to show a comparison and contrast between the Jewish-Christian and Greek understandings of God. Having made this connection, he went further to present Christ as the man who will "judge the whole world with justice" (Acts 17:31).

In review, Christian leaders in the early church used Scripture with their Gentile audiences to provide some historical background and to show the connection between Jesus and Judaism. We see that the early Christian Church is portrayed by Luke as a Christ-directed, Spirit-empowered church, that worshiped God through prayer and the use of Scripture.

5. Fellowship. Were there other elements of worship besides prayer and Scripture? Yes, *fellowship* seemed to have played an important role in early church worship. Luke makes special mention of fellowship in the early days of the church (2:42, 44). Times of fellowship also seem implied in other parts of Luke's historical account (see 2:46–47; 4:32–35; 5:42; 9:31, 43; 10:48; 12:12; 13:43; 14:21–22, 28). Paul's meetings in Philippi (16:15, 33, 34, 40) and his farewell time with the leaders of Ephesus (20:36) are especially good examples of the close fellowship some of the early believers enjoyed.

6. Music. Another element of worship is *music*. The only specific example Luke gives is of Paul and Silas "praying and singing hymns to God" in jail at Philippi (16:25). But with the rich poetic and musical heritage reflected throughout the Old Testament, it is difficult to imagine the early Christians as a non-singing people.

The Old Testament is filled with music. From the mention of "Jubal, the ancestor of all musicians who play(ed) the harp and the flute" (Genesis 4:21); to the songs of Moses and Miriam (Exodus 15:1–21); to David with his harp and psalms; right down to Jesus who led His disciples in a hymn on the night before He was crucified (Matthew 26:30); it is difficult to imagine Christians experiencing Pentecost and not breaking into song over and over again.

> The Comforter has come! The Comforter has come!
>
> The Holy Ghost from heav'n,
> the Father's promise giv'n.
>
> O spread the tiding 'round, wherever man
> is found—The Comforter has come![31]
>
> *Frank Bottome (1823–1894)*

7. Communion. *Communion or the Lord's Supper* was another component of worship that seems to be implied by Luke's phrase, "they had their meals together" (2:46). In fact, the Living Bible translates this phrase as "They . . . met in small groups in homes for Communion . . . ." The seriousness of Paul's discussion of communion in 1 Corinthians 11:17–34, leads to the conclusion that the Lord's Supper was an important part of early Christian worship.

8. Baptism. A final element of early Christian worship was *baptism.* In our time, baptism can be a complicated, theological subject. There are debates on whether infants should be baptized or only adults who confess Christ as their Savior. There are debates about whether baptism is symbolic or sacramental and whether there should be baptism for the dead. Luke presents a much simpler picture of baptism. First he acknowledged John the Baptist's important ministry as recently remembered (Acts 1:5; 9:1–4). In his report of Peter's Pentecost Day sermon, it seems that a mass baptism took place for those who repented of their sins (2:38, 41). As a result of

Philip's revival in Samaria, others who "believed Philip's message about the good news of the Kingdom of God and about Jesus Christ . . . were baptized, both men and women" (8:12). Even Simon, the magician, believed and was baptized (8:13), as was an African government official (8:36–39). They even baptized Saul, the terrible persecutor of Christians, when he changed his attitude and behavior (9:18).

Luke recorded other baptisms also—in Caesarea at Cornelius's house (10:48), in Philippi down by the riverside (16:14–15), and at the jailer's house (16:31–33). When Paul arrived in Ephesus, the believers had already been baptized (19:1–3), and Paul recalled his own baptism in his testimony outside of the temple (22:16). Luke's last record of a baptism was in Corinth, where Crispus, the synagogue leader, and "many other people," who heard and believed Paul's message, were baptized (18:8).

What do we see in Luke's records of early church baptisms?

- We see that water baptisms in Acts were a continuation of the Spirit's ministry through John the Baptist (1:5).

- We see that baptisms were usually preceded by a message about Jesus Christ.

- We see that baptism usually came at the beginning of a believer's Christian experience and was followed by Christian nurture (2:41–42). Verse 42 says that those who were baptized, "spent their time in learning from the apostles, [and] taking part in the fellowship . . . ."

- We see that baptism was often a "family affair" (10:24, 47–48; 16:15, 33; 18:8).

- We see that baptism was an "equal opportunity experience" for all believers—regardless of gender (8:12, "men and women"), race (10:1, 48, Cornelius was a Gentile), or national origin (8:27–28, an official from Ethiopia).

Summary. Worship in the early Christian Church of Acts was much like worship in our Christian churches today. It is probably more structured now, more consistent from church to church, and more elaborate in terms of worship places, equipment, and clothing. But the basic elements of prayer, Scripture, fellowship, music, communion, and baptism were present then as they are now. Regardless of the poverty or richness of our worship setting, the Lord is still seeking persons to worship Him "in spirit and in truth" (John 4:24, KJV).

12
A Ministering Church

O Master, let me walk with Thee
in lowly paths of service free;
tell me Thy secret, help me bear
the strain of toil, the fret of care.

Help me the slow of heart to move
by some clear, winning word of love;
teach me the wayward feet to stay
and guide them in the homeward way.

Teach me Thy patience, still with Thee
in closer, dearer company,
in work that keeps faith sweet and strong,
in trust that triumphs over wrong.

In hope that sends a shining ray
far down the future's broadening way.
In peace that only Thou canst give
with Thee, O Master, let me live.[32]

Washington Gladden (1836–1918)

We have looked at Luke's portrait of Peter and Paul, and have already discussed their various ministries, including speaking, healing miracles, organizing, evangelizing, fund-raising, and writing. In this chapter, we want to focus on two other ministries—ministry of judgment and the ministry of encouragement.

A. Ministry of Judgment

Luke is a rather positive Christian historian and is considered by some to be idealistic. He is not generally a bearer of bad news and evil tidings. But it is hard to overlook those passages where he records episodes of judgment.

The first is the story of Ananias and Sapphira—how chilling. They were two people, husband and wife, dead in church on the same day, in the same place, for the same crime against God—conspiring to lie and cheat (Acts 5:1–11).

The second bone-chilling episode is in Samaria. Luke tells us that Philip, one of the preaching deacons, was in town conducting a very successful revival. One of the persons who got saved was Simon, a magician. He was simply overwhelmed by the miracles the Lord was working through Philip and later through Peter and John (8:6–14). And when he saw that people were receiving the Holy Spirit as Peter and John laid their hands on them, he could not restrain his enthusiasm and offered them money for some of their power (8:18–19). Well, Peter "went off" and said, "May you and your money go to hell, for thinking that you can buy God's gift with money!" (8:20). It seems that Peter really overreacted, especially in light of his own pre-Pentecost record of cussing and cutting (Matthew 26:69–74; John 18:10). However, perhaps Peter's indignation was "righteous," not personal. Anyway, he composed himself and told Simon to repent. He did and asked Peter and John to pray for him (Acts 8:22–24).

The third bone-chilling judgment-episode was the death of Herod. The Herod mentioned in Acts 12 is one of the six Herods mentioned in the New Testament. The first was *Herod the Great,* who was in power when Jesus was born and was responsible for the murder of the boy babies in and around Bethlehem (Matthew 2:1–7, 13–18). The second Herod was *Herod Philip I,* who was responsible for the death of John the Baptist (Matthew 14:1–12). The third was *Herod Antipas,* the one to whom Pilate sent Jesus to be tried (Luke 23:6–12). *Herod Philip* was the fourth Herod. He was the founder of Caesarea Philippi. Luke mentions him in Luke 3:1. Another Herod was *Agrippa II,* the one before whom Paul made his speech in Acts 25 and 26. His son, *Herod Agrippa I* is the person about whom Luke wrote in Acts 12.[33]

Luke is a skillful storyteller and sets the emotional tone for Herod's horrible death by showing us what kind of person he was. For no lawful reason, Herod started persecuting the church, and then killed the apostle James, John's brother. When Herod saw that the Jews liked what he had done, he decided to arrest Peter, put him on trial, and probably planned to kill him too (12:1–5). But the Lord stepped in and miraculously delivered Peter from jail (12:6–11). When the guards couldn't find Peter, Herod had them killed (12:18–19).

For some reason that Luke does not tell us, Herod was angry with the people of Tyre and Sidon, two cities north of Palestine. It seems that they were dependent on Herod for food supplies and knew how evil Herod could be. So they influenced Blastus, Herod's chief of staff, to get them an appointment to plead with Herod for peace. They also knew how vain Herod was and decided to appeal to his vanity by calling him a god. Herod was "eating it all up" when God sent an angel who struck him with a sickness that filled him with maggots. He died because he accepted the people's worship instead of "giving the glory to God" (12:23, LB).

A final episode of judgment happened as Paul, Barnabas, and Mark began their first evangelistic tour (13:1–12). They were sent by the Antioch church and sailed from Seleucia to the island of Cyprus. Sergius Paulus, an especially intelligent government official who lived in Paphos, wanted to hear the Word of God, so he sent for the evangelists.

Bar-Jesus or Elymas (his Greek name) was a magician and one of Paulus's assistants, but he kept interrupting, to keep Paulus from hearing Paul's message and "trusting the Lord" (13:8, LB). Luke reports that Paul finally looked Elymas straight in the eye, called him a "son of the devil" (13:10, LB), and cursed him in the name of the Lord and the power of the Holy Spirit. Immediately Elymas went "blind as a bat." Sergius Paulus was flabbergasted (v. 12, "amazed," NIV; "astonished," KJV, LB) at the judgment miracle. He believed the evangelists' message, and Paul and his party sailed on to the next stop in Turkey (v. 13, LB).

What important messages was Luke trying to communicate by including these spine-chilling stories in his "History of the Early Christian Church"?

1. They were true ministries, done by God directly or indirectly

under the guidance and power of the Holy Spirit. The crucial ministry-question is: Was anybody helped? In each case, Luke adds a qualifying phrase after the episode. After the death of Ananias and Sapphira, the church was helped (see 5:11, 14), and Simon the magician was helped to see his "mistake" and asked for prayer (8:24). After Herod's death, Luke said, "The word of God continued to spread and grow" (12:24). And after Elymas's blindness, Sergius Paulus believed (13:12).

2. Luke helps us to see that the apostles did not use their gifts of power for their personal benefit. . . . Neither Peter nor Paul was ego-tripping. They were acting on behalf of God, under the power of the Holy Spirit. When Peter was speaking to Ananias, he asked, "Why did you . . . lie"—not to Peter or even to the church but—"to the Holy Spirit?" (5:3). Peter said to Simon the magician, "Your heart is not right in God's sight" (8:21, emphasis added). Luke reported, "The angel of the Lord struck Herod down, because he did not give *honour to God*" (12:23, emphasis added). Elymas was struck with blindness because he kept "trying to turn the Lord's truths into lies" (13:10). These acts were not personal vendettas but acts of God, using the apostles as His instruments.

3. Luke helps us see that the primary focus of these acts of judgment was not the people involved but Satan, who motivated their actions. Peter asked Ananias, "Why did you let *Satan* take control of you and make you lie . . . ?" (5:3, emphasis added). He said to Simon, "I see that you are full of bitterness and captive to *sin*" (8:23, NIV, emphasis added). Herod's actions spoke clearly about who he was working for (12:1–3, 19). In the case of Elymas, Luke reported that Paul called him, "You son of the *Devil!*" (13:10, emphasis added). In the truest sense, the focus of the judgment was Satan. Ananias, Sapphira, Simon, Herod, and Elymas suffered because they were Satan's agents.

4. Luke shows us that God is merciful, but we cannot deliberately oppose Him and expect to successfully escape His condemnation or punishment. If we willingly sin or deliberately go against

God's program or God's people, we might receive mercy, as some of the people of Corinth did when "they opposed (Paul) and said evil things about him" (18:6). But Luke includes these episodes to let us know that we can't take God's mercy and patience for granted. He might not strike us down or call us into account. But ask Ananias, Sapphira, Herod, or Elymas; they will tell us not to count on it.

B. The Ministry of Encouragement

In a real sense, Luke's books of "Gospel" and "History" are a lasting part of his ministry of encouragement. How is it possible for Christians to read the triumphs of Jesus Christ and His church and not be encouraged? The Holy Spirit is a comforter, a counselor, and encourager (John 14:16, 18, 26). Peter and Paul were men of encouragement and Barnabas, a prominent "minor" character's name meant "One who Encourages" (Acts 4:36).

1. Encouraging Events. Luke begins his book with at least three encouraging events. First he alludes to the Resurrection—a very crucial and encouraging event without which there would be no Christian Church. During Jesus' last days on earth, during His trials, torture, and crucifixion, His disciples were understandably very discouraged. They had left their families, occupations, friends, homes—everything—to follow Jesus. And now He is being terribly mistreated and finally He is dead. One of the most unbelievable and encouraging events in their lives happened on "Easter" morning.

Second, Jesus didn't rise from the dead and leave immediately. No, He spent at least 40 days with the disciples, appearing "many times in ways that proved beyond doubt that he was alive" (1:3). How encouraging! The third encouraging event was the Ascension! It can hardly be said that the disciples were glad to see Him go, but it seems that since He insisted on going, it was encouraging to see Him "taken up to heaven" with two men in white promising them that He would return (1:9–11). They were also encouraged by His words as they thoughtfully walked the six blocks back to Jerusalem and up the steps to the second story room. That's where

Jesus told them to wait for the baptism (1:5) and power (1:8) of His Spirit, the Holy Spirit. What a tremendous boost to their courage when Jesus sent His Spirit, just as He said He would. PENTECOST no longer meant the celebration of an ancient custom, it now meant a fulfillment of Jesus' promise to be *with* them, *on* them, and *in* them. How encouraging!

We could now look at the apostles' preaching, teaching, and miracle-working as ministries of encouragement. We could see the early Christians worshiping, fellowshiping, sharing, and growing as responses to encouragement. But we have already discussed these topics under other headings. What we want to give our attention to now are Luke's references to specific instances of encouragement throughout his "History of the Early Christian Church."

2. Barnabas, "One Who Encourages." The first use of the term "encouragement" is in connection with Barnabas. By his act of generosity, he encouraged others to share their possessions. Luke wrote that Barnabas "sold a field he owned, brought the money, and handed it over to the apostles" (4:37). Barnabas also exercised his ministry of encouragement when Paul was first introduced to and rejected by the Jerusalem disciples. Paul had treated Christians so badly that even the apostles "were all afraid of him" and could not believe that he was now a disciple of Christ (9:26). So "Barnabas came to his [aid] and took him to the apostles," recounted his Damascus experience, and explained to them that he was now preaching "in the name of Jesus" (9:27). Luke closes this section by writing, "Through the help of the Holy Spirit [the church] was strengthened and grew in numbers, as it lived in reverence for the Lord" (9:31). How encouraging.

Barnabas's ministry of encouragement was also demonstrated in Antioch (11:19–23). Because of an outbreak of persecution connected with Stephen's death, some believers went to Antioch and began preaching to Gentiles about Jesus. Many people believed and were saved. So the Jerusalem church sent Barnabas to Antioch as their ambassador. "When he arrived and saw how God had blessed the people" there, Luke said that "he was glad and urged (encouraged) them all to be faithful and true to the Lord with all their hearts" (11:23). Then Luke, who greatly admired Barnabas, added this wonderful description: "Barnabas was a good man, full of the Holy Spirit and faith, and many people were brought to the Lord [through him!]" (11:24).

But Barnabas had not finished his ministry of encouragement. Next he went to Tarsus, Paul's hometown, and brought him back to Antioch. He encouraged Paul to help the saints there by using his gift of teaching. Luke reports, "For a whole year the two [Paul and Barnabas] met with the people of the church and taught a large group" (11:26). Isn't it wonderful that Barnabas was available to encourage Paul, the apostles, and the church?

3. The Encouragement "Caravan." In Antioch of Pisidia, Luke records one of Paul's major sermons. He also notes that Paul and Barnabas *"encouraged"* those who believed "to keep on living in the grace of God" (13:43, emphasis added). Later they went back to Lystra, Iconium, and Antioch of Pisidia where they had witnessed earlier. There, "They strengthened the believers and *encouraged* them to remain true to the faith" (14:22, emphasis added).

4. Encouragement for Gentile Christians. It was the testimonies of Peter, Paul, and Barnabas that encouraged the apostles in Jerusalem to "not trouble the Gentiles who [were] turning to God" (15:19) with a lot of Jewish rules, rituals, and ceremonies. The recounting of the experiences of these missionaries encouraged the apostles not to insist that Gentiles become Jews before they could become Christians. It was the Holy Spirit working through Peter, Paul, and Barnabas that encouraged the Jerusalem Council to open the doors of the kingdom and let the Gentiles come directly to Jesus by faith. It was a source of encouragement and strength when the prophets Judas and Silas carried the apostles' letter to Antioch (15:32).

5. Another Encouragement Caravan. Because of the decision of the apostles in Jerusalem, Paul and Silas were able to say to the Philippian jailer, "Believe in the Lord Jesus, and you will be saved—you and your household" (16:31, NIV).

When Paul and Silas were released from prison, they went to Lydia's house and there "spoke words of encouragement" (16:40). After their painful experience in Thessalonica, Berea, and Athens, Paul needed some encouragement. The Lord appeared to Paul in a vision and said: "Do not be afraid, but keep on speaking and do not give up, for I am with you. No one will be able to harm you, for many in this city are my people" (18:9–10).

With those words of encouragement ringing in his spirit, Paul settled down in Corinth for 18 months. He then returned to Antioch of Syria by way of Ephesus, Caesarea, and Jerusalem. Later he "went through the region of Galatia and Phrygia, strengthening all the believers" (18:23). Luke also notes that Apollos was helped by Priscilla and Aquila and in turn "was a great help to those who through God's grace had become believers" (18:27).

In chapter 19, Paul was back in Ephesus. This time there was a riot. Paul would most likely have been killed, had he gone to the coliseum. But the Ephesian believers "would not let him" (v. 30). After the city clerk "was able to calm the crowd" (v. 35) and send them home (v. 41), Paul called the believers together "and with words of *encouragement* said goodbye to them" (20:1, emphasis added). He then went through the regions of Macedonia and "*encouraged* the people with many messages" (20:1–2, emphasis added). Paul must have loved the Ephesian believers in a special way. In chapter 20, he sent for the Ephesian elders. He knew that this was the last time he would see them, so in his "farewell sermon," he encouraged them with these words: "So keep watch over yourselves and over all the flock which the Holy Spirit has placed in your care. Be shepherds of the church of God, which he made his own through the blood of his Son. Watch, then, and remember that with many tears, day and night, I taught every one of you for three years. 'And now I commend you to the care of God and to the message of his grace, which is able to build you up and give you the blessings God has for all his people'" (20:28, 31–32).

Paul said a few more words, and knelt down with them and prayed. They cried, hugged and kissed him, went with him to his ship, and said a final good-bye (20:36–21:1). It was a heartrending experience, but it must have been especially encouraging for Paul. He was accustomed to being beaten and abused, but this is the only time Luke records such an outpouring of heartfelt love and affection for him. Undoubtedly he was also encouraged, when after a taxing sea voyage, the Jerusalem "believers welcomed [him and his party] warmly" (21:17). How good he must have felt when "they all praised God" (21:20) after he had given his "report of everything that God had done among the Gentiles through his work" (21:19).

Unfortunately, Paul didn't have much time to feel good. In about a week (21:27), some more Jewish troublemakers were on his trail, and a mob was screaming, "Kill him!" (v. 36). And in the next section of Luke's record, Paul is defending himself in front of Jewish mobs and Roman rulers (22:1–26:32).

6. Encouragement at Sea. The next recorded words of encouragement came from Paul. He was on a ship moving slowly toward Rome. He had encouraged the ship captain not to sail because of impending bad weather. The captain ignored Paul's advice and encountered a terrible storm. As the storm was in the process of demolishing the ship, the Lord sent an angel with some encouraging words for Paul: "Don't be afraid, Paul! You must stand before the Emperor. And God in his goodness to you has spared the lives of all those who are sailing with you" (27:24).

Paul, in turn, gave words of encouragement to the sailors: "So take heart, men! For I trust in God that it will be just as I was told" (27:25).

7. Encouragement in Rome. When Paul and his party arrived near Rome, some believers came out to the suburbs to meet them. Luke writes, "When Paul saw them, he thanked God and was greatly encouraged" (28:15, emphasis added).

I remember my father preaching from that text when I was a teenager. I didn't understand it then, but he was probably preaching to himself. He always looked good and talked positive but the 1930s and '40s were stormy times for many people and especially for poor, Black people. The Depression was just ending. Segregation was still the order of the day. Lynching of Black men was brutal and frequent. Some people at the church Daddy pastored were making his life a living hell. We were on the brink of World War II. And so I remember his sermon title: "Thank God and Take Courage."

That's still an appropriate message, isn't it? We have so much for which to give thanks. James Weldon and John Rosamond Johnson expressed it for us so well:

"God of our weary years,
God of our silent tears,
Thou who has brought us thus far on the way;
Thou who has by Thy might
Led us into the light,
Keep us forever in the path we pray."[34]

Yes, "the Lord has brought us from a mighty long way" and we ought to love Him, serve Him, and give Him praise. But we've also got to take courage, haven't we?

Our churches are getting larger; our schools are becoming more violent. Our middle- and upper-class African Americans are making more money, living in better houses, and driving bigger cars; but our unemployment and welfare rolls are getting longer. We have more people in prison and more people living on the streets. We have more people (not just African Americans) who are victims of child abuse and spousal abuse, as well as nicotine, alcohol, and illegal drug abuse. Young people in gangs are shooting each other down in the streets, and in the "red-light districts," there is traffic in female and male bodies as young as 12 years old. If that is not enough to discourage us, then we are reminded of the rise of the Moral Majority, the National Rifle Association, the Skinheads, the American Nazi Party, and the Ku Klux Klan.

Yes, Paul and Daddy, we still need to "take courage!" Perhaps David had the right idea. It is said, "David encouraged himself in the LORD his God" (1 Samuel 30:6, KJV). Aha! That is the secret to a life of courage! The apostles, Barnabas, Aquila, Priscilla, and Apollos were sources of encouragement. But Rome was a long way from Jerusalem, Antioch, and Corinth. The saints in Ephesus were a wonderful source of love and strength, but Ephesus, and Rome were a great distance apart. And so what did Paul do? He "took courage." He was encouraged when he saw the Roman Christians. He didn't wait for their words; he encouraged himself "in the Lord."

That's the key phrase—"in the Lord." Friends and acquaintances come and go, but the Lord is always present. Didn't the Lord say, "Never will I leave you; never will I forsake you" (Hebrews 13:5, NIV)? So in spite of all the things around us and within us that could discourage us, we will encourage ourselves in the Lord—the *word* of the Lord, the *work* of the Lord, and the *worship* of the Lord. Like Paul, we will thank God and take courage!

Having taken courage, Luke reports that Paul went on to Rome, and though still a prisoner, he rented a place and, "He preached about the Kingdom of God and taught about the Lord Jesus Christ, speaking with all boldness and freedom" (28:31).

How encouraging!

13

An Expanding Church

The Lord is in the business
of making things grow.

He told the creatures
of air, sea, and Earth
to bring forth
after their kind,

Adam and Eve,
He told to be fruitful
and multiply.

Abraham's descendants,
He promised to make numberless
like the sand and stars.

The Lord is in the business
of making things grow.

A. The Church Before Pentecost

The Christian church as presented in the New Testament began with one Person, Jesus Christ. He expanded it to 13 persons by choosing 12 men as disciples (Matthew 10:1). Later, He called and sent out another 72 men (Luke 10:1), which increased the number to 85. Luke lists three women, Mary Magdalene, Joanna, and Susanna, who followed and served Him, along with "many other women" (Luke 8:2–3). How many—10? Fifteen? Twenty? Let's estimate 15 to arrive at an approximate number of 100. At the time of Jesus' crucifixion, two of Jesus' secret disciples—Nicodemus and Joseph of Arimathea—"came out of the closet" (John 19:38–40). Along with Jesus' mother and brothers (Acts 1:14), Joseph-Barsabbas, and Matthias, that brought the number to the "about

120" that Luke said gathered in the Upper Room before Pentecost (1:15). So even before their special awareness of the Holy Spirit, Jesus' disciples had increased 10 times their original number.

B. The Jerusalem Church

After Peter's sermon on Pentecost Sunday, the number increased by 3,000 (2:41), and after the healing-of-the-lame-man sermon, the number of believers "reached a new high of about 5,000 men!" (4:4, LB). If we calculate about the same number of women (that calculation is low, if today's American Christian church is an indication of ratios), we have a membership of at least 10,000 people. At this point, Luke stopped reporting numbers and began to use phrases such as "the number of disciples kept growing" (6:1), and "the number of disciples in Jerusalem grew larger and larger" (6:7). Can we modestly estimate the Jerusalem Church to be about 12–15,000 persons?

C. The Samaritan Church

After Deacon Stephen preached his powerful sermon (7:1–53) and was stoned to death, Luke pictured the church suffering "cruel persecution" and being scattered throughout the various towns and cities of Judea and Samaria. With the exception of the apostles, many believers left Jerusalem and "went everywhere, preaching the message" (8:4). Luke then gives an example of the impact of the message by telling of the ministry of Deacon Philip. He went to a large city in the Samaritan area. We are not told how many people were saved, but Luke uses such phrases as "there was great joy in that city" (8:8) and those who "believed Philip's message about the Good News of the Kingdom of God and about Jesus Christ . . . were baptized" (8:12). Peter and John left Jerusalem to go down and give the Samaritan church their blessings (8:14). They were so inspired that they preached on the way back to Jerusalem (8:25).

In the meantime, an angel of the Lord instructed Philip to leave the Samaritan revival to go and minister to an African official on his way back from Jerusalem to Ethiopia (8:26–38). A little later Philip mysteriously found himself in Azotus and Caesarea (8:40). Would it be immodest to estimate the number of converts from the Samaria campaign to be about 2,000 converts?

In chapter 9, Luke tells us of Saul's conversion experience. Even though he began to preach in Damascus (9:20, 22), and to preach, talk, and dispute about Jesus in Jerusalem (9:28–29), Saul was not yet ready for his mission. At this point, he was basically just frightening the believers and making the disbelieving Jews angry. The Greek-speaking Jews got so angry "they tried to kill him" (9:29). So some of the believers "hustled" Paul down to Caesarea and sent him back home to Tarsus (9:30). In his summary report, Luke said: "And so it was that the church throughout Judea, Galilee, and Samaria had a time of peace. Through the help of the Holy Spirit it was strengthened and grew in numbers, as it lived in reverence for the Lord" (9:31).

In the meantime Peter "travelled everywhere" (9:32), primarily in Judea. It was at this time that he visited and ministered to the people of Lydda and Sharon, towns near Jerusalem. We don't know how many lived in these two towns, but Luke reported that after the healing of Aeneas, "they [all] turned to the Lord" (9:35). And when the Lord used Peter to bring Dorcas back to life in Joppa, "many people believed in the Lord" (9:42). People were also saved, baptized in water, and filled with the Spirit when Peter traveled to Cornelius's house in Caesarea (10:1–48).

D. The Antioch Church: The Church Expands North

The church in Antioch began as believers fled from the persecution that was going on in Jerusalem. The result was "a great number of people believed and turned to the Lord" (11:21). Barnabas arrived sometime later and as a result of his ministry "many [more] people were brought to the Lord" (11:24). In the meantime, the Jerusalem Church was still being persecuted, this time by Herod, who had killed James (John's brother). In the last part of chapter 12, Luke reports that Herod, died a horrible death, but "the word of God continued to spread and grow" (12:24).

E. From Antioch to Rome: The Uttermost Parts

Luke's "History" is divided into two major sections. The first part is Acts 1–12 and focuses primarily, but not exclusively, on Peter and the Jewish Church. The second part of Acts (13–28) is centered around Paul and his ministry to the Gentiles. So the remaining part of this chapter on the early church's expansion will center around the three missionary journeys or evangelistic tours of Paul, and will note how the Church expanded north and west from Antioch to Rome.

1. Paul's First Evangelistic Tour. During this tour, Paul and Barnabas traveled to Cyprus, Perga, Antioch in Pisidia, Iconium, Lystra, and Derbe. On the island of Cyprus, Barnabas's home (4:36), two important things happened: (1) Saul began using his Roman or Gentile name Paul, and (2) at least one convert was won to Christ—Sergius Paulus, a Roman government official. In Perga, no evangelistic activity is recorded, but Luke reports that Mark left the team and "went back to Jerusalem" (13:13). Paul preached and taught in Antioch in Pisidia. The Jews rejected his message, but the Gentiles who "wanted eternal life, believed" and "God's message spread all through that region" (13:48–49, LB). In Iconium, "a great number of Jews and Gentiles became believers" (14:1), and in Lystra there were at least enough converts present to gather around Paul after he had been beaten and dragged out of town (14:20). Paul and Barnabas preached in Derbe and "won many disciples" (14:21). They then went back to the cities they had visited to strengthen and encourage the new believers "to remain true to the faith" (14:22), and returned to their home church in Antioch in Syria.

2. Paul's Second Evangelistic Tour. On Paul's second missionary journey, Silas accompanied him. They traveled through Syria, Cilicia, back to Derbe, Lystra, and Iconium and on to Troas, Philippi, Thessalonica, Berea, Athens, Corinth, and Ephesus. It was in Lystra that Paul found Timothy, who joined them on their tour (16:1–4). Luke notes that the churches they revisited "were made stronger in the faith, and *grew in numbers every day*" (16:5, emphasis added).

In a vision while in Troas, Paul received a call for help from Macedonia (16:9). We know of at least three converts in Philippi: Lydia, the fortune telling slave girl, and the Roman jailer (16:14–16,

18, 32–34). Around this nucleus, their families and households developed the church to which Paul wrote one of his most beautiful letters—the Letter to the Philippians. In Thessalonica, a church was established through Paul's teaching ministry (17:1–4). The Thessalonian church was composed of both believing Jews, and "many of the leading women and a large group of Greeks who worshiped God" (17:4).

Paul and his companions traveled on to Berea where the people in the synagogue "listened to the message with great eagerness" and "many of them believed" (17:11–12). In Athens, Paul spoke before the city council, and though there was no great revival, "some men joined him and believed (17:34). Luke noted for special mention a member of the council named Dionysius and a woman named Damaris (17:34). Paul, along with Aquila and Priscilla, Timothy and Silas, stayed in Corinth at least 18 months "teaching the people the word of God" (18:11). Many people "heard the message, believed, and were baptized" (18:8).

3. Paul's Third Evangelistic Tour. After a trip through Ephesus, where he left Aquila and Priscilla, Paul traveled back to Jerusalem and Antioch of Syria and went back through the Galatian and Phrygian regions "strengthening all the believers" (18:23). He began his third missionary journey in Ephesus. He "went into the synagogue and . . . spoke boldly . . . about the Kingdom of God" (19:8) and received his usual rejection by the Jews. But during his two-year stay, Luke reported that "all the people who lived in the province of Asia, both Jews and Gentiles, heard the word of the Lord" (19:10). In verse 20, Luke added that after the great book burning, "the word of the Lord kept spreading and growing stronger." After the Ephesus riot (19:21–41), Paul went back through Philippi, Troas, and Miletus. It was there that he met with the leaders of the Ephesian church, said good-bye, and went on to Jerusalem by way of Cas, Rhodes, and Patara, making stops at Tyre, Ptolemais, and Caesarea.

In a sense, Paul's arrival in Jerusalem ended his third evangelistic tour and was the launching pad for his trip to Rome. Paul was determined to preach in Rome (19:21). He was not the first to introduce Jesus to the citizens of Rome, but the Lord granted his desire to preach there. A group of Roman believers met him at the Forum on the Appian Way, about 40 miles from Rome, and another group joined them 10 miles later at the Three Taverns.

F. Analysis

So what shall we say about the expanding church? First, we see it expanded *numerically*. Even before it officially reached outside of Jerusalem, Luke tells us that the church had grown from the 120 persons in the Upper Room to at least 5,000 men (4:4), 10,000 if we include an equal number of women. If we estimate 2,000 converts in Judea and Samaria; add another 1,000 in Lydda, Sharon, and Joppa; and another 2,000 members in the Antioch (Syrian) church, we have a modest estimate of 15,000 members before Paul began his evangelistic tours. Paul made at least 23 stops. If we added another 10,000 converts won during Paul's three evangelistic tours, it would bring our estimated total to about 25,000 converts. The actual numerical growth was probably 10 times our modest estimate. Remember, all other evangelistic activity did not cease while Paul took the message of Jesus' love and power on his evangelistic tours. By the time Paul arrived in Rome, there were probably half a million Christians. Twenty centuries later, there are over one billion.[35]

In addition to numerical growth, the church also expanded *geographically,* just as Jesus said it would (1:8). Luke recorded that the church began in Jerusalem and within about 30 years (A.D. 30–60), the Gospel had been carried as far north as Bithynia and Pontus (2:9; 1 Peter 1:1), as far south as Ethiopia (Acts 8:39), and as far west as Rome and perhaps Spain, as well as to many islands of the Mediterranean Sea.

The church also grew *organizationally.* In the Upper Room were Jesus' disciples, some of Jesus' family, and some other folk, none with official titles or job descriptions. Later, some of them became teachers (2:42), deacons (6:1–6), evangelists, such as Stephen (6:8) and Philip (8:5; 21:8), and prophets, such as Agabus

(11:28; 21:10–11). In addition, church leaders were appointed to be shepherds of believers in local churches (14:23; 20:17, 28, 31).

In addition to expanding numerically, geographically, and organizationally, the church grew in *diversity.* At first, the church was composed exclusively of Jewish men (Matthew 10:1), but by the time Paul reached Rome, Luke carefully noted along the way that the church included women (1:14; 5:14; 8:3, 12), Africans (8:27; 13:1; 18:24), Greeks (11:20; 14:1; 17:4, 12), Samaritans (8:4–25), and Romans (10:1; 13:12; 28:15, 24). Persons also were included from the society's upper (17:4), lower (3:8–10; 16:16–18) and middle (10:1; 16:27–31) classes. The early Christian Church was a study in diversity, a "rainbow coalition." Was Peter aware of the tremendous truth he quoted from the prophet Joel? "*Whosoever* shall call on the name of the Lord shall be saved" (2:21, KJV, emphasis added).

Finally, the church grew *spiritually.* Luke reminds us many times that as the church expanded in other ways, it was also strengthened (2:42, 46–47; 4:31–32; 5:12–16, 29, 40–42). Luke's picture of early church expansion is a portrait with many colors, textures, and perspectives. The central focus of the portrait is Jesus Christ, our Saviour, our Lord, our Friend. Because of the church's focus on Him, it "kept spreading [wider] and growing stronger" (19:20).

14

The Model Church: First Century Lessons For The Black Church Of The Twenty-First Century

Are there lessons that the Black Church can learn from the first century Christian Church? If so, what are they?

A. The Excitement of a Single Focus

The central focus of the early church was Jesus Christ. Plans, programs, and personnel, as well as buildings, membership, and organizations are important; but those were not the central concerns of the early church. The first century Church was focused on Jesus Christ. Luke writes in the first few verses of Luke and Acts that his purpose was to report what Jesus began to do and teach. He achieved his purpose by focusing his books on the life and ministry of Jesus, from His birth to the testimony of Paul about Jesus in Rome. It's an exciting and inspiring story that illustrates the power of a central focus.

The Black Church has many tasks. It must reach and influence Black *and* White communities. The church is our foundational community institution and our only hope of survival and success. It must cooperate with and help all of the other organizations of positive influence. It must work with the NAACP, SCLC, Rainbow/PUSH, the American Red Cross, American Cancer Society, Diabetes Hope Foundation, and other religious, economic, social, and political organizations. But if it is to stand true to its primary spiritual calling and have the power to influence political, economic, and social change, Jesus Christ must be its central focus. Our community has many persons who have been crippled from birth by the effects of slavery, discrimination, and social neglect, as well as personal negative habits and wrong decisions. No amount of medical, financial, social, or political assistance will meet their basic need. Like the man at the Beautiful Gate (Acts 3:1ff.), if they are to ever function "normally" as persons and citizens, they need a miracle. The Black Church can be an exciting place of deliverance and restoration only as it keeps its focus on Jesus Christ. Many of our communities need a daily barrage of miracles. Keeping our central focus on Jesus Christ is our exciting challenge and hope.

> On Christ the solid rock (we) stand;
> All other ground is sinking sand.[36]

B. The Effectiveness of Evangelism

The growing churches in the Black community are the churches that evangelize. The consistent words of Jesus to His disciples were "come" and "go." In Mark 1:17, Jesus said to Peter and Andrew, "Come with me." Later, He said to Matthew, "Follow me" (Mark 2:14). He invites us to come and learn (Matthew 11:28–29), but never to stay. The next call is to "go" (Matthew 10:5–15; Mark 6:7–13; Luke 9:1–6; John 20:21; Acts 1:8). The "secret" of the rapid growth and influence of the early church was its evangelistic activities. Notice it was not just the apostles (the clergy) who evangelized, but also "ordinary" believers who "went everywhere, preaching the message" (Acts 8:4). The churches in Samaria, Damascus, and Antioch were not planted by the apostles, but by "ordinary" believers through whom God did extraordinary things (8:5; 9:10, 19–21).

There are those who are announcing the ineffectiveness and coming demise of the Black Church. These uninformed persons must not have visited Black churches like Big Bethel AME Church in Atlanta, Georgia, or West Angeles Church of God in Christ in Los Angeles, California. These are only two of the many outstanding Black churches in the United States; there are many others that are evangelizing their communities. Black churches are also expanding in Africa, England, the Caribbean, and Australia. The Black Church is very much alive. And wherever evangelism is taking place, people are being added to the Church in significant numbers.

Are we doing enough evangelizing? No. As long as there is one drug addict, one prostitute, one thief, one rapist, or one carjacker in our neighborhood or *any* neighborhood, we have not evangelized enough. Should we expect that every person to whom we witness will be saved? No, Paul was rejected by some in Antioch of Pisida, Iconium, Lystra, Derbe, Thessalonica, Berea, Athens, and Rome. But others "were convinced" and became followers of Jesus Christ (17:4). No matter how often and intensely the Black community (or any community) is evangelized, every person will probably not become a Christian. Jesus didn't win Judas, who was with Him every day for at least two years. But if we emphasize evangelism as did the first century Christian Church (some of whom were Black—Acts 8:27–39; 13:1), we can make a significant and lasting impression for good on our people.

C. The Emphasis on Holistic Ministry

Matthew reported that "Jesus went all over Galilee, teaching . . . preaching . . . and healing . . ." (Matthew 4:23; see also 9:35). Jesus ministered to whole persons—mind, spirit, and body. In Acts, the apostles and other Christian leaders carried on this same mode of ministry. Not only did Peter and the apostles preach to win "souls" for Christ, they also healed bodies (Acts 3:1ff.; 5:12–16; 8:4–8), carried on a teaching ministry (2:42; 11:25–26; 28:23), and set up "programs" for sharing food and other resources (2:43–46; 4:32–37; 6:1–6; 11:27–30). Some of the most inspiring preaching in the world goes on in the Black Church. The whole world got a little "taste of it" during the mid-fifties and sixties from the challenging and uplifting messages of Dr. Martin Luther King Jr.[37] We must preserve and encourage "good" preaching. There is nothing like an effective Black preacher who knows how to "tell the story" and to make it relevant to our personal and collective circumstances. Excellent Black preaching (as well as White, Red, and Yellow) can actually lift people out of their seats mentally and physically, change their attitudes, and affect their behavior for the rest of their lives (Romans 1:16).

We must not discourage good Black preaching, but we must add a greater emphasis on teaching. Peter encouraged his readers to grow in grace *and knowledge* (2 Peter 3:18). Increasingly, progressive Black churches are leading the way in buying or building church properties that include classrooms and other educational facilities. They are also adding Christian educators to their staffs and including larger allocations of funds in the budget for teaching-learning activities.

There seems also to be a greater emphasis on health concerns—both in terms of "faith healing" and the promotion of health maintenance by "Health-day" screening programs and exercise programs. There is a growth in activities and ministries that are concerned with victims of excessive smoking, alcohol, and drug abuse, and AIDS. Many larger Black churches have groups that minister to the needs of people in hospitals, senior citizen homes, youth detention centers, orphanages, jails, and prisons. Through the early Christian Church in Acts, Jesus ministered to people who were in need. We must continue to do the same, and to accelerate and intensify our efforts.

D. The Beauty of Teamwork

Isn't it interesting that Jesus never tried to be the Lone Ranger without taking along Tonto? In both the Gospel accounts and through the believers in Acts, the emphasis of Christian ministry is team ministry. Jesus seldom went anywhere without His disciples, and when He sent the 72 disciples to minister, He sent them by twos (Luke 10:1). Luke records that on the Day of Pentecost when Peter preached his 3,000 member sermon, he was standing "with the other eleven apostles" (Acts 2:14). When the Lord sent Peter to Cornelius, he was sent as a team member (10:23). And from the record, it seems that while Philip went to Samaria as an individual, his ministry was not complete until members of the team were sent to join him (8:14–17). Remember when Paul when on his evangelistic tours, he was accompanied by Barnabas (13:2–3), Silas (15:40), Timothy (16:3–5), Luke (16:10–11), or Priscilla and Aquila (18:18). Jesus, Peter, and Paul were definitely leaders—*team* leaders.

Hopefully, this 21st century will find our cities with fewer storefront churches lined up side by side with one preacher and six members each, and more churches with several preacher-leaders under one roof with a cooperative spirit and program of quality ministry to the people in the neighborhood. We don't want to disparage small ministries, because just as oak trees grow from acorns, so too do many large ministries begin as small assemblies, and sometimes very small assemblies.

What we *do* want to advocate is that every person who feels called to be a pastor should not feel that he or she has to be in charge of his/her own church. Great businesses, corporation, schools, and governments are the result of many competent people working together. So it is that great churches are also the result of "prophets . . . evangelists . . . pastors and teachers" (Ephesians 4:11), and other workers cooperatively providing quality ministry for a community. The addition of a competent assistant, or associate or copastor can greatly enhance the effectiveness of a church's ministry. Team ministry is one of the "secrets" of the first century Christian Church that the Black Church can "discover" and imitate.

E. The Necessity of Organization: The KISS Principle

Have you heard about the five-word note the visiting preacher received from his wife? It said, "KISS—KEEP IT SIMPLE, SWEETIE! Now, there is a version where the last word is "stupid," but that is not our version. She affirms him and encourages him to do well. Her note, KEEP IT SIMPLE, SWEETIE, was her way of affirming him and encouraging him to communicate effectively by not displaying all of his accumulated wisdom at one time.

This KISS principle was demonstrated by the early church as a organizational technique. They didn't make their organizational form fit into it. They organized "as they went." They made their organization form fit the church's function. They didn't have an alternate disciple in case Judas committed suicide. They only elected Matthias because Judas's place was vacant (Acts 1:14–26). They didn't set up a "deacon board" until there was a need (6:1–6). Paul and Barnabas appointed elders when there were churches that needed them (14:23). This is not a plea for less long- and short-range planning.

We are not advocating a "seat of the pants" or "shoot from the hip" church management style. We are saying that it is possible to spend too much of our resources on layers of paper shufflers and not enough on Christian education and training programs that prepare people to do ministry. It is possible to spend too much of the church budget on *maintenance instead of ministry.* We need to be sure not to spend more of the church's resources of time, energy, and money on the comfort of the saints rather than the mission of the church to sinners. Is our priority worship and other church programs for the churched, or evangelism and outreach to the *unchurched?*

The 21st century is becoming increasingly well organized, with a balanced allocation of resources for worship, Christian education, evangelism, community social services, and world missions. In the 21st century the Black Church has more people and more resources involved in more types of ministries at home and abroad. One of our challenges is to remember the KISS principle.

F. The Strength of Unity

Does Luke portray a rosy picture of the church? Was everything wonderful, blissful, and great? Did all the believers spend "their time in learning from the apostles, taking part in the fellowship, and sharing in the fellowship meals and the prayers" (Acts 2:42)? The answer is "yes"—at the beginning. But did conflict raise its head? Were Ananias and Sapphira real people (5:1–11)? Was there "a quarrel" between the Greek-speaking Jews and the native Jews (6:1–6)? Was there a "fierce argument" between the Judaizers and the "saved by grace" groups (15:1–2, 11)? Was there a "sharp argument" between Paul and Barnabas (15:39)?

Everything was not "sweetness and light" in Acts. These early Christians were real folk, with real diversities of perspectives, opinions, and convictions. But by God's wisdom and grace, even though they argued and debated, judged (5:4–10), decided (6:2–4; 15:19–21), separated, and reconciled (15:36–41; 2 Timothy 4:11), they carried the Gospel from Jerusalem to Rome and were accused of turning "the world upside down" (Acts 17:6, KJV).

As our clergy and laity become more educated and affluent, our churches will experience more diversity of perspectives, opinions, and convictions—with louder expressions of dissent. As the problems outside of the Church multiply, the pressure on the Church for solutions will intensify. The Church, especially the Black Church, will be less able to hide its head in the sands of spirituality. It will be called upon for positive involvement in such issues as abortion, child and spousal abuse, and crime—both street and white collar. Prayerfully the amount and intensity of discussion in the Church will increase, and the number and diversity of solutions will escalate. Such debate is to be encouraged because historically, any permanent, positive advance—social, political, or economical—has come from the Black Church directly or through its influence. The 21st century Black Church must participate seriously and enthusiastically with other community groups and welcome diversity of opinions and actions. At the same time it must attend to its primary spiritual functions of reaching people for salvation, teaching them for spiritual growth, and recruiting, preparing, and enlisting them for church, community, and world service.

To effectively meet its many challenges, the Black Church must unite with other religious groups—churches, synagogues, cathedrals, and mosques—and other community, social, political, and economic organizations with compatible purposes. The problems and needs of the Black community are so deep and broad that the Church cannot afford to even try to meet them unaided. If the Black Church is to help turn our world right side up, it must do its spiritual task AND form alliances with other groups that are sincerely trying to make a positive difference in the quality of our people's lives.

At this crucial time in the history of the church, we cannot afford fighting between denominations. Liberals and conservatives must struggle together against racism, sexism, and classism. We cannot afford to ignore or rant and rave against the religions of the world. We cannot afford to spend time and energy "dissing" our public schools and sending our politicians to hell. We must welcome those who are genuinely concerned—from every nationality. The challenges to the Black Church are colossal, but they are no greater than the challenges were to the first century Church. Their "secret weapon" and ours is the same—UNITY—with Christ and with each other. A phrase from Paul's second letter to the Corinthians might well be our motto: "We then, [are] workers together with him" (6:1, KJV). And our theme verses might be: "God in his mercy has given us this work to do, and so we are not discouraged. In the full light of truth we live in God's sight and try to commend ourselves to everyone's good conscience. There are many enemies, but we are never without a friend" (2 Corinthians 4:1, 2, 9).

G. Don't Forget to Laugh

Is it by accident that Luke included some genuinely funny incidents in his serious account of the Church's expansion from Jerusalem to Rome? There is a note of humor in the story of the apostles' miraculous escape from jail (Acts 5:18–19). One day they were put in jail; the next day when the officials came to bring them before the Jewish Council, they found the cells locked, guarded, and *empty.* They were advised that the apostles were carrying on a Bible class in the temple. Can you see the "red" faces and feel the embarrassment of the big, tough Council officials (5:20–26)? Did Luke have a smile on his face as he wrote about the evil spirit running the sons of Sceva out of their clothes (19:11–20)? Can you hear the restrained smirk in Luke's voice as he told his friends back in Jerusalem about how Paul preached so long that Eutychus went to sleep and fell out of the window (20:7–12)?

The Black community has very serious problems both internally and externally. It must deal with these challenges by employing all of its resources, both human and divine. But it must not become so engrossed in the gravity of its task that it loses its ability *to laugh, to sing, to shout, to dance.*

It was Nehemiah who reminded his newly liberated people, "The joy of the Lord is your strength" (Nehemiah 8:10, KJV). In the world of the 21st century, we need all of the strength we can find. So we must maintain our joy—our ability *to laugh, to sing, to shout, to dance.* We must keep on singing our spirituals and gospel songs, raising our hands in praise and clapping them with enthusiasm. We must not stifle the drums or muzzle the organ, trumpet, and saxophone. We must not attempt to silence the tambourine or stop the tapping feet. We must not sober the smiling faces or muffle the hallelujahs; for the joy of the Lord is our strength. We must not lose our ability *to laugh, to sing, to shout, to dance.*

The joy of the Lord brought us through slavery, through lynchings, through denial of the right to read, write, and vote. We sang, shouted, clapped, and danced our way through defeat and death into victory and freedom. In the 21st century, let's keep our joy and appreciate the level of intensity with which each of us desires to express it. We dare not encourage the frivolous, the indecent, the silly, or the irreverent, but neither will we trade the refreshing waters of spontaneous worship for the deadening swamps of religious formality.

We will not imprison the songbirds of our joy within the cage of our church walls. We will take our joy into the streets where we walk, the homes where we rest, the schools where we study, the offices, and shops where we work, the banks where we save, and the malls where we spend. Our joy will infect those we meet and they will join us in our gladness as we go into the house of the Lord. We will teach them to *laugh, to sing, to shout, to dance.* Our joy will strengthen us to pray, to study, and to work for our God, ourselves, and our people.

Lift ev'ry voice and sing
Till earth and heaven ring,
Ring with the harmonies of Liberty;
Let our rejoicing rise
High as the list'ning skies,
Let it resound loud as the rolling sea.
Sing a song full of the faith that the
dark past has taught us,
Sing a song full of the hope that the
present has brought us,
Facing the rising sun of our new day begun,
Let us march on till victory is won.

God of our weary years,
God of our silent tears,
Thou who has brought us thus far on our way;
Thou who has by Thy might
Led us into the light,
Keep us forever in the path we pray.
Lest our feet stray from the places, Our God, where
we met Thee,
Lest our hearts drunk with the wine of the world, we
forget Thee,

Shadowed beneath Thy hand,
May we forever stand.
True to our God, true to our native land.[38]

NOTES

INTRODUCTION

1. *Luke's Portrait of Jesus* is a companion to this volume. (Chicago: Urban Ministries, Inc., 1993).

ACTS, BOOK OF HISTORY

2. For information regarding the titles of Acts, see Willie Marxsen, "The Acts of the Apostles," *Introduction to the New Testament,* translated by G. Buswell (Philadelphia: Fortress Press, 1968), 167. Also see James Orr, John L. Nuelsen, and Edgar Y. Mullins, eds., *The International Standard Bible Encyclopedia,* Vol. 1 (Peabody, Mass.: Hendrickson Publishers, 1994), 39; and Ralph Earle, "The Book of Acts," in *Adam Clarke's Commentary on the Bible,* abridged (Grand Rapids, Mich.: Baker Book House, 1983), 956.

3. I. Howard Marshall, *The Acts of the Apostles* (Grand Rapids, Mich.: Eerdmans Publishing Co., 1980), 48.

4. William Robertson, *Studies in the Acts of the Apostles* (New York: Revell, n. d.), 5.

5. Ralph Earle, ed. "Pentecost and Missions (Acts), *Exploring the New Testament* (Kansas City, Mo.: Beacon Hill Press, 1955), 230, 238, 243.

LUKE, THE WRITER

6. Most of the information for this chapter is taken directly from our book, *Luke's Portrait of Jesus.* In our research we did not discover any new information of significance. We are repeating here what we discovered previously.

7. G.B. Caird, *The Gospel of St. Luke* (Philadelphia: Westminster Press, 1963), 16.

8. Albert Barnes, "The Gospels," *Barnes' Notes on the New Testament* (Grand Rapids, Mich.: Kregel Publications), iii.

9. For more information on the "we" passages, see: Balmer H. Kelly, Donald Miller, Arnold B. Rhodes, eds., "Luke," *Layman's Bible Commentary,* Vol. 18, (Atlanta: John Knox Press, 1959–64), 24. Donald Juel, *Luke–Acts: The Promise of History* (Atlanta: John Knox Press, 1983), 6.

10. Caird, 16.

11. *Ibid.,* 17.

12. Barnes, 1. Also see: Caird, 15; Miller, 25; and William Barclay, *The Acts of the Apostles* (Philadelphia: Westminster Press, 1976), 1.

13. Barnes, 1.

14. Caird, 15.

15. Barclay, *The Acts of the Apostles.*

16. I. Howard Marshall, *Luke: Historian and Theologian* (Grand Rapids, Mich.: Zondervan Publishing Company, 1971), 25.

17. Barclay, *The Acts of the Apostles,* 1–2

PORTRAIT OF PETER: A BIOGRAPHICAL SKETCH

18. B. Van Elderen, "Peter, Simon," *The Zondervan Pictorial Encyclopedia of the Bible,* Vol. 4, ed. Merrill C. Tenney (Grand Rapids, Mich.: Zondervan Publishing Company, 1975), 738.

PORTRAIT OF PETER: A CHARACTER SKETCH

19. Frederick Faber (words) and Henri Hemy (music), "Faith of Our Fathers," *Yes, Lord!* (Memphis, Tenn.: Church Of God In Christ Publishing Board, 1982), 27.

PORTRAIT OF PAUL: A BIOGRAPHICAL SKETCH

20. John Hayes, *Introduction to the Bible* (Philadelphia Westminster Press, 1971), 391.

21. J. L. Kelso, "Trade, Commerce and Business," *The Zondervan*

Pictorial Encyclopedia of the Bible, 5 Vols., ed. Merrill C. Tenney (Grand Rapids, Mich.: Zondervan Publishing Company, 1976), 790.

22. Herbert Lockyer, *All the Men of the Bible* (Grand Rapids, Mich.: Zondervan Publishing Company, 1958), 270.

23. R. N. Longenecker, "Paul, the Apostle," *The Zondervan Pictorial Encyclopedia of the Bible,* 5 Vols., ed. Merrill C. Tenney (Grand Rapids, Mich.: Zondervan Publishing Company, 1976), 625.

24. *Ibid.,* 650, 654.

PORTRAIT OF PAUL: A CHARACTER SKETCH

25. Douglas Malloch, "Be the Best of Whatever You Are," http://poetryarchive.bravepages.com/IKLM_poets/malloch-douglas.html.

THE MINISTRY OF PETER AND PAUL

26. *Ibid.,* 631–632.

27. Barclay, *The Acts of the Apostles,* 22–24.

28. Earle, *Exploring the New Testament,* 227–259.

THE CHRIST-DIRECTED CHURCH

29. Fanny Crosby, "Tell Me the Story of Jesus," www.digitalhymnal.org/dhymn.cfm?hymnNumber=152.

A SPIRIT-EMPOWERED CHURCH

30. Earle, "The Book of Acts," 956.

A WORSHIPING CHURCH

31. Frank Bottome, "The Comforter Has Come!" *Precious Times of Refreshing and Revival,* 1890.

A MINISTERING CHURCH

32. Washington Gladden, "O Master, Let Me Walk with Thee," www.hymnsite.com/lyrics/omh430.sht.

33. Barclay, *The Acts of the Apostles,* 93–94.

34. James Weldon Johnson and John Rosamond Johnson, "Lift Every Voice and Sing," 1899, www.africanamericans.com/ NegroNationalAnthem.htm.

AN EXPANDING CHURCH

35. Barclay, *The Acts of the Apostles,* 22–24.

THE MODEL CHURCH: FIRST CENTURY LESSONS FOR THE BLACK CHURCH OF THE TWENTY-FIRST CENTURY

36. Edward Mote (words) and William Bradbury (music), "The Solid Rock," *Yes, Lord!* (Memphis: Tenn.: Church of God in Christ Publishing Board, 1982), 13.

37. For a collection of Dr. King's printed sermons, see *Strength to Love* (Philadelphia: Fortress, 1988). For an audiocassette of some of his speeches and sermons, see "Dr. Martin Luther King Jr.: Speeches and Sermons" (Martin Luther King Foundation, 309 East 90th Street, New York, NY, 10028).

38. James Weldon Johnson and John Rosamond Johnson, "Lift Every Voice and Sing," 1899, www.africanamericans.com/ NegroNationalAnthem.htm.

BIBLIOGRAPHY

Barclay, William. *Acts of the Apostles.* Philadelphia: Westminster Press, 1976.

————. *The Gospel of Luke.* Philadelphia: Westminster Press, 1975.

Barnes, Albert. "The Gospels." *Barnes' Notes on the New Testament.* Grand Rapids, Mich.: Kregel Publications, reprinted from the 1884–85 edition.

Blaiklock, E. M. "Acts of Apostles." *The Zondervan Pictorial Encyclopedia of the Bible.* Vol. 1, Grand Rapids, Mich.: Zondervan Publishing Company, 1975.

Brown, C. "Day of the Lord (YAHWEH)." The Zondervan Pictorial Encyclopedia of the Bible. Vol. 4, Grand Rapids, Mich.: Zondervan Publishing Company, 1976.

Cadbury, H. J. "Acts of the Apostles." *The Interpreter's Dictionary of the Bible.* Vol. 1. Edited by George A. Butterick and Keith R. Crim, 1986.

Caird, G. B. *Saint Luke.* Philadelphia: Westminster Press, 1963.

Carter, Charles. "The First Church Was Led by the Holy Spirit." *Pulpit Help,* January 1995, 23–24.

Dean, Robert, ed. *A Study Guide to Acts.* Nashville: The Sunday School Board of the Southern Baptist Convention, 1972.

Earle, Ralph. "The Book of the Acts." *Adam Clarke's Commentary on the Bible* (abridged). Grand Rapids, Mich.: Baker Book House, 1967.

Goodwin, Bennie. "The Acts of the Apostles." *The New Testament Story.* Atlanta: Goodpatrick, 1992.

————. *Luke's Portrait of Jesus.* Chicago, Ill.: UMI (Urban Ministries, Inc.), 1993.

Grogan, G. W. "Baptism for the Dead." *The Zondervan Pictorial Encyclopedia of the Bible.* Vol. 1. Grand Rapids, Mich.: Zondervan Publishing Company, 1976.

Harris, R. L. "Luke's Gospel." *Your Bible.* Wheaton, Ill.: ETTA, 1986.

Hayes, John H. *Introduction to the Bible.* Philadelphia: Westminster Press, 1971.

Headlam, A. C. "Acts of the Apostles." *Hastings' Dictionary of the Bible.* Vol. 1. Peabody, Mass.: Hendrickson Publishers, 1989.

Irwin, C. H., ed. *Irwin's Bible Commentary.* Grand Rapids, Mich.: Zondervan Publishing Co., 1979.

Jewett, P. "Baptism (Baptism View)." *The Zondervan Pictorial Encyclopedia of the Bible.* Vol. 1. Grand Rapids, Mich.: Zondervan Publishing Company, 1976.

Juel, Donald. *Luke–Acts: The Promise of History.* Atlanta: John Knox Press, 1983.

Kistemaker, Simon. *New Testament Commentary: Acts.* Grand Rapids, Mich.: Baker Book House, 1990.

LePeau, Phyllis. *Acts: Seeing God's Power in Action.* Downers Grove, Ill.: InterVarsity Press, 1992.

Longenecker, R. N. "Pauline Theology." *The Zondervan Pictorial Encyclopedia of the Bible.* Vol. 4. Grand Rapids, Mich.: Zondervan Publishing Company, 1976.

———. "Paul, the Apostle." *The Zondervan Pictorial Encyclopedia of the Bible.* Vol. 4. Grand Rapids, Mich.: Zondervan Publishing Company, 1976.

Marshall, I. Howard. *Luke: Historian and Theologian.* Grand Rapids, Mich., Zondervan Publishing Company, 1971.

———. *The Acts of the Apostles.* Grand Rapids, Mich.: Eerdmans, 1980.

Martin, William. "Paul." *The Layman's Bible Encyclopedia.* 1964.

Marxsen, Willi. "The Acts of the Apostles." *Introduction to the New Testament: An Approach to Its Problems.* Translated by G. Buswell. Philadelphia, Fortress Press, 1980.

Miller, Donald. "The Gospel According to Luke." *The Layman's Bible Commentary.* Vol. 18, Louisville, KY.: Westminister, John Knox Press, 1982.

Munck, Johannes. "The Acts of the Apostles." *The Anchor Bible.* New York: Doubleday Books, 1967.

Murray, J. "Baptism Reformed View." *The Zondervan Pictorial Encyclopedia of the Bible*. Vol. 1. Grand Rapids, Mich.: Zondervan Publishing Company, 1976.

Neyrey, Jerome, ed. *The Social World of Luke–Acts: Models for Interpretation* Peabody, Mass.: Hendrickson Publishers, 1991.

Ogilvie, Lloyd. *Acts: Mastering the New Testament. (The Communicator's Commentary Series, Volume 5)*.Waco, Tex.: Word Books, 1979.

Robertson, William. *Studies in the Acts of the Apostles*. New York: Revell, 1901.

Roth, R. P. "Baptism (Sacramentarian View)." *The Zondervan Pictorial Encyclopedia of the Bible*. Vol. 1. Grand Rapids, Mich.: Zondervan Publishing Company, 1976.

Slemming, Charles. "Acts of the Apostles: Begun and Continued." *The Bible Digest*. Grand Rapids, Mich.: Kregel Publications, 1960.

Van Elderen, B. "Peter, Simon." *The Zondervan Pictorial Encyclopedia of the Bible*. Vol. 4. Grand Rapids, Mich.: Zondervan Publishing Company, 1976.

White, Jr. W. "Synagogue." *The Zondervan Pictorial Encyclopedia of the Bible*. Vol. 5. Grand Rapids, Mich.: Zondervan Publishing Company, 1976.